"WOULD YOU PLEASE SAY A FEW WORDS?"

by NORMAN NEL

Copyright® 1998 Executive Living (Pty) Ltd

All rights reserved

No part of this publication may be reproduced, stored in a retrieval system or transmitted, in any form or by any means, electronic, mechanical, photocopying, recording or otherwise, without the prior permission of the Publisher.

Cover Design by Jet Set Photosetting (Pretoria)
Edited by Christine Pulvermacher, Cape Town
Illustrations by André de Beer
Reproduction by Jet Set Photosetting
Printed by CTP Book Printing (Pty) Ltd
Published by Executive Living (Pty) Ltd,
PO Box 95756, Waterkloof 0145

ISBN 0-620-22730-3

DEDICATION

I dedicate this book to my grandchildren, Lexi, Oliver and Marcus, in the hope that they will one day excel in the art of communication. Their enthusiasm for life knows no bounds and their expression of love, hope, wants and desires are so natural and uninhibited that any orator who takes lessons from them, can only succeed.

COMPANY CEO

"Any person occupying a seat of success – at any level, will inevitably be called upon to 'say a few words'. When that time comes, this book is a must whether it be for a small circle of fiends or an illustrious international audience. Good luck!"

FORMER DIRECTOR OF CULTURAL AFFAIRS

"This book is welcomed with great enthusiasm. It contains valuable quotations, wonderful ideas and jokes that will entertain any audience. The author displays a remarkable ability to skillfully change attitudes from despair to optimism in a style and language that everyone can relate to. Highly recommended."

CAREER DIPLOMAT

Undoubtedly a Great Read! "If I had had a book like this one, the many invitations over the years to 'Say a few words' on dozens of occasions, would not have bothered me. The emergence of this book has been long overdue. It's an absolute gem!"

NATIONAL SPORTS ADMINISTRATOR

"The author is vastly experienced in many spheres of life. Despite not having the full use of both legs and having been educated at a remedial school, his positive attitude has enabled him to outshine his peers in whatever he has tackled. This remarkable book displays a relaxed style, unique sense of humour and it will entertain young and old alike.

During his career he has addressed hundreds of gatherings all over the world with ease, authority and conviction. 'Would you please say a few words' is a tonic for any speaker in our global village. I strongly recommend it."

RETIRED ATTORNEY

"The author, as is evidenced by this book is a man who, when applying his mind to personal, political, religious or sport topics, emerges as a very special person. His objective to create a book that will help and guide the occasional speaker, has certainly been achieved. Well done!"

ACKNOWLEDGEMENTS

To the many people who have encouraged me to complete this work – thank you. In particular, André de Beer for your excellent illustrations – you have made this book a work of art; Christine Pulvermacher for editing; Peter Good for your practical ideas and for writing the foreword; Dawie Pretorius for coming to the rescue whenever it was necessary; Erna Fivaz for typing the manuscript, and Peter Beaton for your excellent suggestions and practical comments.

FOREWORD

True art, it has been said, is the art that conceals art. And the truth of this pithy epigram is perhaps never more evident than when it comes to making a speech or euphemistically put, "saying a few words". When Ernie Els hits a golf ball it looks easy. When a good surgeon performs an operation, it also looks easy. And when a good speaker "says a few words" it looks as if anybody could do it.

Norman Nel, the author, has overcome innumerable physical disadvantages in his life and generally succeeded in turning his disabilities into advantages. He has unquestionably succeeded in becoming an excellent (and most sought after) speaker.

While there are numerous books which purport to teach one how to construct speeches, how to prepare them, or what to say, there are very few "Source Books" available containing speech material which is directed at being helpful or inspirational. This book, being a compendium of suggestions, speeches and particularly anecdotes, is not only an enjoyable read but also an invaluable tool which will be most useful to all persons required from time to time to make speeches.

"Would you please say a few words?" will fill a deserved place in any library both as light reading and instruction.

Peter Good

TABLE OF CONTENTS

1. INTRODUCTION 1

2. SPEECH OPENERS AND CLOSERS 9
   - Introduction for a talk on building confidence 9
   - Introduction for a talk to a group of businessmen 10
   - Church gathering 11
   - Chamber of Commerce 11
   - Chairman or President's dinner 12
   - Substituting a speaker at short notice 12
   - Impromptu 13
   - A portrait of the economy 13
   - Humorous opener 14
   - The Queensbury Rules 15
   - After a very flattering introduction 16
   - Technical subject to a knowledgeable audience 16
   - Politics a call for action 17
   - Setting the example 17
   - Thanks 18
   - Inspirational 18
   - It's up to you 19
   - Motivational 20
   - Big business is small business with an extra nought ... 20
   - A tree bearing fruit 21
   - Humorous close 22

- Get yourself steamed up 22
- Education and planning 23
- You can if you think you can 24
- You can't if you think you can't 25
- What motivates you? 25
- Agricultural society 26

3. SAMPLE SPEECHES 29
   - Standing Ovation 29
   - Motivation and a time for change 45
   - Don't wait – do it now? 48

4. COMMENCEMENT SPEECHES 57
   - Matric farewell 57
   - Commencement address 61
   - Rules of the game 64

5. THE WORLD AROUND US 69
   - South Africa today 69

6. BIRTHDAYS 77
   - My very special friend 77
   - The metallurgical age 78
   - Seventy something 79
   - Heaven's very special child 80
   - Any age 81
   - 85 years young today 81

7. GOLDEN OLDY TRIVIA 87
   - Evolution as a monkey sees it 87

INDEX

- Methuselah 88
- An 85-year-old, dying from cancer 88
- Age is a quality of the mind 89
- Youth and age 89
- The preservation of man 90
- Yes, I'm tired 90
- When are you old? 91
- How do you know when you are growing old? 92
- Remember 93
- At day's end 93
- A touch of wickedness 94
- It's all in your mind 95
- I am fine 97

8. EULOGIES 101
   - Eulogy to Roger Boustred 101
   - Eulogy to Pat McGrath 102

9. INSPIRATIONAL STUFF 107
   - A toast 107
   - When God gave out brains 108
   - Time to pray 108
   - Footprints in the sand 109
   - Statement of faith 110
   - The sermon on the mount 110
   - The golden thread 110
   - Heaven's grocery store 111
   - What is charity 112
   - An Irish blessing 113
   - Dear friend 113

- Limits of parenthood 115
- Children live what they learn 116
- Mothers' day 116
- Isn't life glorious 117

10. SUCCESS 121
- What success is all about 121
- Succeed with E's 126

11. SUCCESS TRIVIA 129
- The guy in the glass 129
- The four senses of success 130
- A simple formula for success 130
- Don't quit 130
- Sailsman sole them half a million 131
- A smile 132
- If you are unhappy 132
- Are you a salesman? 133
- See the people 133
- The indispensable 133
- The Salesman 134

12. PETTY TRIVIA 139
- Good stuff 139
- Irish General Certificate of Education 1998 139
- Heaven is where 140
- African definitions for health terms 141
- A survivor's guide to SABC TV pronunciation 142
- Dear white fella 143

INDEX

13. COMPANY TRIVIA 147
  - A secretary's prayer 147
  - Thought for the day 148
  - Advertising that works 148
  - Risk 149
  - Mark Twain's view 150
  - Everybody, somebody, anybody and nobody 150
  - Staff announcement 151
  - Guide to safe fax 151
  - What not to call your dog 152
  - Which are you? 153
  - Political philosophies 154
  - Different kinds of buyers 154
  - Answer me 155
  - Men are four 155
  - The why check-list 155
  - Real Estate 156
  - Working days in the New South Africa 157
  - A great man must be mindful of nine things 157

14. PRESENTATION SPEECH 161

15. AFTER DINNER 167
  - Say it with flowers 171

16. WEDDINGS 175
  - An old Indian Legend 175
  - Genesis 2: 18 – 24 177
  - The first letter of St. Paul to the Corinthians 177
  - The Lord's commandments 178

- Climate clash 178
- The art of marriage 179
- The marriage check-list 179
- Nothing suited him 180
- Toast to the parents of the bride 180
- Toast to the parents of the groom 181
- Toast to the bride and groom 182
- The best man's speech at a wedding 182
- The bridegroom 183
- The speech 183
- Translated from A.G. Visser 184
- A bride's prayer 185

17. JOKES 189
- Never lose your head for a bit of fluff 189
- Doctor 189
- Pistol whistle 190
- Different generations 190
- Stop drinking 191
- Mistakes 191
- What's wrong 191
- Drop your pants 192
- It doesn't matter where you hide it 192
- Veterinary science 193
- Bank managers 193
- Kiss your mother-in-law 194
- Construction man 194
- Lawyers 194
- Happily married 196
- Lead in his pencil 196
- Courting humour 196

INDEX

- Too tense 197
- A peer in the pot 197
- Frenchmen 198
- So extravagant 198
- The Rottweilers 198
- Artichokes 199
- To whom it may concern 200
- Grandpa 200
- No culture 200
- Blame the Government 201
- Getting cleverer and cleverer 201
- Ordered radio by mail order 202
- I didn't know you were so religious 203
- I prayed for you last night 203
- Introducing the bridegroom 204
- Teaching my wife to drive 204
- Tarzan 204
- Matrimonial argument 205
- Talking balls 205
- Politics 205
- Two seater 206
- Get the wrong idea 206
- Property 207
- Require testimonials 207
- Rectum thermometer 207
- Cannot bear a child 207
- Insurance 208
- The private sector 208
- The law protects you 208
- No last words 208
- Mothers 209

- Such a small thing 209
- Slowing down 209
- Get thee behind me, Satan 210
- True love 210
- Lawyer 210
- Potential millionaire 210
- What do we need Dad for? 211
- Evolved from apes 211
- Bridegroom's love 211
- Swop 212
- Angel 212
- Chains of wedlock 212
- Finished 212
- In heaven 213
- Suicide 213
- Hanging around 213
- Just married 213
- Paint the town 214
- Insignificant detail 214
- Mothers-in-law 214
- Pigeon turpie 214
- Decisions 215
- Marry me 215
- Last word 215
- It balances out 215

CHAPTER ONE

INTRODUCTION

INTRODUCTION

Coming from Africa I have no fear of lions, elephants, snakes or spiders. However, ask me to propose a toast, make a speech or be master of ceremonies at a wedding... and I am gripped by fear. My knees register nine on the Richter scale, I get butterflies, my lips start quivering as if to cry and my brain goes numb.

Fortunately, most invitations to perform these duties are not impromptu, they usually give one a few months notice. Regardless, I have learned that even the best impromptu speeches take a few weeks to prepare, so don't be fooled by the seemingly composed speaker who is able to handle any situation at the drop of a hat.

This book is the product of an idea that started a few years ago, when, once again, I was asked to say a few words. Once more, I had to find material, something new, something different to say, which would *please* and *entertain* the audience. I wondered why there were so few books available for a layman speaker like myself. A book containing sample speeches for social and other occasions. A collection of speech introductions and closures that would prepare an audience for the body of a talk or leave them on a 'high' at the end of it. Perhaps even a few good jokes.

A stockpile of ideas to refer to – a book for business leaders and professionals, ordinary people who are so often called upon, (sometimes at short notice) 'to say a few words'. I realise that a professional speaker develops the ability to speak because it is worthwhile, and once developed, it becomes a valuable asset. This book is not intended to be a handbook for learning to speak in public. At best, it is a convenient collection of sample speeches, quotations, jokes and trivia that may point you in the right direction or assist you to get your talk started or ended. I am no orator and to overcome my fear of speaking in public, I use the power of simplicity, four letter words like life, love, home and wife, which trigger my brain into action. Soon the butterflies are flying in formation, my lips stop making me look a fool and I can control the nervous energy wasted through my knees by using body language.

One doesn't need a large vocabulary, it's not a prerequisite for eloquence, but like drama, painting and music, effective speech is the yardstick of civilisation and there is no reason why one should not manage with a small word stock.

H. Phelphs Gates sums it up beautifully when he says:
There is a strength and force in short words: words that blast and boom, throb and thump, clank and chime, hiss and buzz and zoom. There is grace and charm in short words too, in words like lull and purr. There are short harsh words like dank and drench; and short dry ones like crisp, parch and husk. There are words that work hard at their job, that pry and push, that slash and hack, that cut and clip, that chip and saw...

He ends with this tribute to words that sell:
... Scan the best sales jobs in print and you'll find them rich in short words that tease the taste, make glad the eye, wet the nose, and please the ears. They're sweet, tart, or dry as the need be. There are words you can hear like the swish of silk; soft words with the feel of swansdown; words with a smell like musk, smoke, cheese, mint, and rose – all of them good sales tools. Yet oft as not in talk or script we'll force the use of some long hard word, and with it, blunt the keen edge and dull the sharp point of what we want to say...

Preparing to speak in public requires suitable material, and finding it is much the same as digging for diamonds. At first we dig around in the yellow clay where we may find a gem or two, but it's only by digging deeper into the blue ground where the real gems are, that we discover our greatest rewards. *Would you please say a few words* is a collection of material researched over 40 years that will make your delving much easier.

CHAPTER ONE

This book is filled with dozens of ideas and paging through it will provide material that will make speeches sparkle. Without deviating from the focus, let me touch on a few basic principles of speaking that are not intended to be instructive but merely guidelines to settle the nerves.

Humour plays an important role, it endears the speaker to his audience and it builds confidence. The Golden Rule is always, *keep it clean.* A clever joke has a double meaning ie the audience may *think* it is naughty, but you must never remove all doubt. This book also contains good, clean jokes for all occasions, every one of them can be told in public. Before telling a joke in public, you must *convince yourself* that it is funny, understand the punch line and remember that surprise is the secret of a good laugh. Once you have selected a joke, practise it on someone until you get it right.

THE VOICE

Some people have natural handicaps, such as high-pitched voices, imperfect articulation or even a nasal twang. If a speech is compelling, all impediments are overlooked.

LANGUAGE

When language gets in your way, don't be discouraged, you can succeed if you speak from the heart.

ATTENTION

It is often said that a speaker succeeds or fails in the first five minutes. This is not always true. But if you can get the attention of your audience in the first five minutes, the chances of success are increased. Remember it takes a cold hammer to bend a hot iron. Heat up your audience, but keep the hammer cold. People love word pictures that excite the imagination and stir the emotions.

INTRODUCTION

By using the material in this book, you can *impress* people, *persuade* them, *motivate* them, *inspire* them, *enrich* them, *convince* them and *direct* them.

One of your objectives must be to endear yourself to your audience through basic human relations. I came across these ten commandments by an unknown author.

1. Bear in mind when speaking to people – there is nothing as nice as a cheery word of greeting.
2. Smile at people – it takes 72 muscles to frown, only 13 to smile.
3. If possible call them by name – the sweetest music to anyone's ears is the sound of his or her name.
4. Be friendly and helpful – if you would have friends, be friendly.
5. Be cordial – speak and act as if everything you do is a genuine pleasure.
6. Be genuinely interested in people – you can like everybody if you try.
7. Be generous with praise – cautious with criticisms.
8. Be considerate for the feelings of others – it will be appreciated.
9. Be thoughtful of the opinions of others – there are three sides to any story. Yours, the other fellow's and the right one.
10. Be able to give service – what counts most in life is what we do for others.

Bear in mind while you are preparing your speech that every house that was ever built looked like a major disaster when it was only half completed. By adding one brick at a time it gradually takes shape and becomes a *home*. A great speech is built one brick at a time.

CHAPTER TWO

SPEECH OPENERS AND CLOSERS

SPEECH OPENERS AND CLOSERS

During the past 40 years I have been called upon hundreds of times to introduce the speaker, deliver the key note address, be master of ceremonies, propose the toast, deliver the eulogy etc., etc. Here are some openers and closers that work. Naturally the names, organisations and characters must be changed to suit your own mission. Most of the material is original, but a lot of it comes from things that I have read, heard or developed.

INTRODUCTION FOR A TALK ON BUILDING CONFIDENCE

When I left the airport this morning, my mind went back to a day in East London a few months ago, when I was boarding an aeroplane for a flight to Johannesburg. The weather was foul and even the birds seemed to be grounded. Having been a pilot myself, I was not unduly worried because I knew that modern aircraft fly high above the clouds at altitudes of ten kilometres and more above sea-level, where the air is smooth and where there is little or no turbulence. I calculated, that within ten minutes we should be above the weather and floating in armchair comfort at great speed towards our destination. But that wasn't to be, because having reached our cruising altitude and been up there for over half an hour, the aircraft was still being tossed around like ice in a cocktail shaker. A glance at my grey, petrified-looking fellow passengers revealed the torment that was going through their minds. Even the cabin crew were strapped in and looking pale!

Suddenly... a calm, confident voice came over the air and said, "Ladies and gentlemen, this is your captain speaking. We apologise for the turbulence and any discomfort it may have caused, but please be assured that this aircraft is designed to fly safely in much worse conditions. We will be leaving the turbulence behind us in a few moments, after which the cabin crew will resume their usual friendly service. Our position is at present overhead Maseru, the capital of the little kingdom in the skies. We will continue at our altitude of 10 000 metres above sea-level for another 20 minutes and thereafter start our descent for landing at Johannesburg International Airport where the weather is fine and the temperature 28°. Our expected time of arrival is on schedule. Please enjoy the rest of your flight."

His voice was confident, calm and reassuring. Soon everyone relaxed and was smiling and chatting away normally, because here was a man on board who knew exactly where we were, at what altitude we were flying, the weather conditions on arrival and also exactly when we would touch down at our destination. Moments later we burst into clear blue skies, just as he had said we would.

I have often wondered what would have happened if the captain had emerged from the cockpit with a parachute strapped to his back, saying, "Don't worry, I'm going for help!"

INTRODUCTION FOR A TALK TO A GROUP OF BUSINESSMEN

Approaching my subject for today's session, I couldn't help thinking of the dignified, carefully groomed man, somewhat grey about the temples, who was walking along by the side of the lake (let us just assume he was a banker). There was no wind and the water was so clear that one could see right down to the bottom. Our banker, however, sees only his own reflection in the water's calm surface. He is so fascinated by his reflection that it does not even occur to him to look beyond it.

And because he just sees that 'highly interesting' reflection, he thinks that what he sees just confirms what he has always known: his 'own reflection' prevents him from seeing into the depths.

CHAPTER TWO

This story is, of necessity, about 'a banker'. However, there is no profession or line of business in which we do not tend to want our own views upheld. This kind of attitude is economically and socially dangerous and untenable. However, as businessmen, we have to look deeply into things, plumb the depths and sound out all the information.

CHURCH GATHERING

They say that you should have your speech well in mind before you start. Well, this one is in my heart and it has been there for a long time. If it does not come out as easily as it should, then please understand it is because it is deeply rooted.

CHAMBER OF COMMERCE

During the last three weeks I have had the opportunity to spend time in New York, Washington, Paris and London, as well as Rome, Venice, Lake Como and Lisbon. I have had the privilege to meet and speak with important people, to see and observe, and sense attitudes at first hand. It is my intention to share some of these experiences and stated opinions with you today. Everything always looks different when you look down the barrel instead of through the sights. In this highly competitive world we live in, we are often on the defensive.

This brings to mind the Duchess of Dorchester, one of the renowned bores and great socialites of the late 19th century. To the annoyance of some, on a special occasion, she found herself seated between Gladstone and Disraeli. Her friends could hardly contain themselves in asking how she found the two distinguished gentlemen, to which she replied that in the early part of the evening, in talking with Gladstone she had been convinced that he was undoubtedly the cleverest and most able man in England. However, when she subsequently had the opportunity to discourse with Disraeli, he had convinced her that she was without doubt the most fascinating woman in all Europe!

SPEECH OPENERS AND CLOSERS

CHAIRMAN OR PRESIDENT'S DINNER

Being chairman has its lighter moments. The other evening at a dinner, a fellow walked up to a lady and said, "Well, if that's Joe Soap, our chairman, then I am terribly disappointed. I expected to see someone far more imposing and intelligent-looking."
The lady stiffened. "I beg your pardon," she said. "That is Joe Soap and do you know who I am?"
He shook his head.
"I am Mrs Joe Soap," she said.
For a moment, he was dumbstruck. But being a good professional, he quickly recovered and asked, "Do you know who I am?"
"I do not," she answered haughtily .
"Thank goodness for that," he said and got up to leave.

In welcoming you this evening, I must say that I feel a little like the mosquito who arrived at the nudist camp. He surveyed the territory and said, "I don't know where to begin ...".

So far, during my term of office, I have had the pleasure of boring quite a few audiences. I have simply ignored the good advice of experienced speakers who say ... if you don't strike oil in the first three minutes ... stop boring. Some of my listeners are quite tactful though ... they tell me afterwards that a speech is like a bicycle wheel ... the longer the spoke, the bigger the tyre.

SUBSTITUTING A SPEAKER AT SHORT NOTICE

When I was at school, a missile shattered a class room window on a Friday afternoon – too late to have it glazed for the weekend. It was in the rainy season and our teacher had to improvise with something else to make sure that if it rained, there would be no damage to the wooden floor. He found a piece of cardboard, cut it to size and made a perfect substitute for the glass pane.

Well, I don't want to be a perfect substitute today, I want to be a real pain.

CHAPTER TWO

IMPROMPTU

I had hoped to escape the watchful eye of the master of ceremonies this evening as I am not trained in the art of making public speeches; but it seems that I have been discovered at the very beginning of this meal. To settle my nerves, I am tempted to tell a story, although I am not sure if it is appropriate.

I heard of a farmer who went to the Rand Easter Show. In the livestock section he noticed some very ordinary cows among some highly pedigreed stock. Very curious, he wondered whether this was another clever marketing ploy, to make the pedigreed stock look much better than they really were. He asked the attendant if that was the reason. "Not at all," replied the attendant. "The ordinary cows are here to provide milk for the pedigreed calves!"

Looking at the number of excellent speakers we have here tonight, I hope that it is not expected of me to provide the entertainment for all the pedigreed speakers.

A PORTRAIT OF THE ECONOMY

An artist sat at a table in his regular restaurant. After dinner, he usually polished off two bottles of his favourite wine. On this occasion, as he was about to order his second bottle, his eye caught a newspaper headline ... *Downturn in the economy predicted.*
He called for his check. "Is there anything wrong with the wine?" the waiter asked.
"No, the wine was excellent but the economy is going to dip and I must conserve my cash," said the artist.
"Difficult times coming?" said the waiter. "Then my wife must not buy that new dress she has ordered." The dress shop accepted the cancellation and decided that this was not a good time to expand the business as it would be better to wait for the economy to improve.

Hearing that hard times were coming, the builder decided that he would no longer be able to have his wife's portrait painted and wrote to the artist accordingly. After receiving the letter, the artist despondently went to the restaurant again. This time, he ordered a small bottle of wine to soothe him. On a nearby table lay the same newspaper in which he had read the bad news a few days before. He picked it up to read more closely, only to find that the newspaper was five years old.

This little story illustrates quite vividly that the greatest danger this country faces is when you and I become despondent and start spreading negative thoughts.

HUMOROUS OPENER

Just before I took the stage, one of the ladies in the audience saw me pacing up and down in a little room somewhere back there. She asked me, "Are you always this nervous before you talk in public?"
"Nervous? Don't be silly, I'm not nervous!" I retorted.
"Then what are you doing in the ladies' bathroom?" she asked. (Allow time for laughter.)

I was guest speaker at a dinner the other night. There was this well-dressed man in evening dress with black tie. I said, "I'm (Piet Pompies)" and shook his hand with all the cordiality I could muster.
"My name is James, Sir, I'm the headwaiter," he replied.
"Let's shake hands again," I said "You don't know how much I envy you tonight."
(Allow time for laughter.)

My wife puts it in a nutshell. At home the other night, I was practising my speech when I asked her, "Darling, do you think I should put more fire into my speech?"
"No!" she said, "but I do think that you should put more of your speech into the fire!"
(Allow time for laughter.)

I am told that the Government has introduced a new form of punishment... you have to listen to after-dinner speakers. (Allow time for laughter, if there is no laughter, just proceed.)

Now that I have your attention, perhaps we can get on with the subject matter that I have been asked to talk about. Ladies and gentlemen, for the next half hour, my job is to talk to you and your job is to listen to me. If you finish before I do, just raise your hand, I catch on fast! (Allow time for laughter.)

THE QUEENSBURY RULES

In the year 1867, the Duke of Queensbury established a set of rules for professional boxing. A Code of Conduct, if you like, wherein the respectability of boxing as a sport was entrenched. This moral code was accepted internationally. Amongst other things, it required a boxer to wear gloves. Each round would last for only three minutes and punching below the belt was outlawed.

After a knockdown, the attacking boxer must immediately return to a neutral corner. Although boxing was considered violent, the rules attracted gentlemen to the sport. With the passage of time, the rules and the morals have survived.

For many years, business was conducted by a set of unwritten rules, very often cemented by a simple handshake. That gut *feeling*, when you could *smell* a deal a mile away, see an opportunity sticking out, *taste* the reward of perseverance and hear the applause for a job well done. The rules were adhered to by everyone, the moral fibre was strengthened and passed on to younger generations, the referee was your own conscience. There is no softer pillow than a clear conscience.

Today, our *sight* seems blurred by bribery and corruption, our nostrils are clogged with the stench of injustice. Our *feeling* of brotherhood is distorted by racial prejudice and our ears are deaf to the calls of reconciliation. Our *taste* for revenge grows stronger with each day and the rules of

Africa seems as harsh as the jungle has ever been. And yet ... when the drums of Africa beat in your veins and the dust of this ancient continent has settled on your soul, you know that we have been put here together for a purpose. Not to be thrown into a crucible or melting pot but to be like a delicious fruit salad, each one retaining his own identity, yet adding to the flavour of the other. We must establish a new set of rules, we must reinforce that moral bond, we must establish a code of ethical conduct that will set South Africans apart from the rest of the world, we must develop pride, and a feeling of belonging that will transcend all prejudice and God willing – we must become good South Africans.

AFTER A VERY FLATTERING INTRODUCTION

Mr Chairman, your introduction today reminds me of an occasion when the Archbishop of Cape Town was being introduced to an audience. The chairman extolled the many virtues of the Archbishop for about 20 minutes, during which time he used many examples of deeds supposedly performed by His Grace. Some of them even surprised the Archbishop himself as he could not recall them. On taking the podium, he said, "Mr Chairman, I don't know who has committed the biggest sin today. You for your generous praise and some use of journalistic elasticity, or me for enjoying listening to it so much".

TECHNICAL SUBJECT TO A KNOWLEDGEABLE AUDIENCE

My dilemma here today in speaking to such a learned audience, is similar to that of Mr van der Merwe who found himself at the Pearly Gates after drowning in the Laingsburg floods. The Archangel welcomed him and said, "We are having a symposium in two weeks time and all the newcomers up here are expected to give a one hour talk on a subject they know well".

Van der Merwe who had just experienced the ravages and devastation of the Laingsburg floods said, "That's no problem, I'll talk on floods!"
"That's all right," said the Archangel, "but do remember that Mr Noah and his family will be in the audience as well".

POLITICS, A CALL FOR ACTION

When you are unhappy about the way your taxes are being squandered, or the way the country is being run, don't wait for someone else, someone more important, to act on your behalf, for if you do, you must ask yourself the question... "who is that person? Is he an important businessman? Is he a member of Parliament? Does he belong to the right political party? And when the time comes, will he act in our best interest?"

Don't find yourself in the position of the defeated politician who, when he was asked about his constituency, said, "My constituents believe in me, they will do anything for me, they will trudge to hell and back for me, they are 100 % behind me".
"So why did you lose the election?" he was asked.
"They didn't vote. Ladies and gentlemen, this is our constituency, this is our election, this is our collective responsibility and each one of us must attend to it personally on election day. I look forward to speaking to each one of you at the polls."

SETTING THE EXAMPLE

Sir Harry Lauder used to tell the story of the lamp lighter in the village where he grew up. The old man would make his rounds with a ladder and his lighter. He would put the ladder against the post, climb up and light the lamp, climb down again and move to the next lamp. After a while, he would be out of sight, so you couldn't see him anymore but you could always see which way he had gone from the lamps he had lit. I believe that this is the greatest tribute that any of us can receive from our fellow citizens. With all my heart, I hope that some of the things that I have said here today, will light a lamp in your heart, but more important, that you will leave this convention convinced that as you walk down the road of life, people will follow your course in the light of the lamps that you have lit for them.

THANKS

I would like to say how much I have personally enjoyed being here. During today's programme, we have on several occasions experienced great moments. Moments that I am sure, will live in our minds forever. We have thoroughly enjoyed listening to the ideas and messages of these truly wonderful people who are prepared to give so much of their valuable time to all of us ... at tremendous sacrifice to themselves, at a time when most people are finding it necessary to spend more time on their own businesses.

I would like to thank all of them and all of you for having brought together a really special group of people... people who are prepared to say "Our cause first!" I know that when we benefit from a seminar, we usually want to come back for more. I also know that this is exactly how you feel today, so let's put our hands together and say to the committee "Thanks a million and please fellows... do it again".

INSPIRATIONAL

In closing, I must urge you to continue with the work you are doing, don't give up! Success comes to those who keep on keeping on. We must take courage from the great artists of the past, to mention only a few, *August Rodin* grew up in absolute poverty, three times his application to be admitted as a student in sculpture was turned down. This exalted artist spent many years earning a meager living, making ornamental decorations for buildings. *Vincent van Gogh* wrote to a friend on one occasion saying my main meal comprises dry bread and chestnuts. Today his paintings are worth millions. *Leonardo da Vinci*, the illegitimate child of a peasant girl was poor, hungry and homeless, yet he became one of the greatest artists that ever lived.

Johann Sebastian Bach, again, as poor as a church mouse and without education, developed into one of the principal composers in the world. We all enjoy his music. *Ludwig von Beethoven* left school at the age of 13 to become the family's breadwinner because his father was an alcoholic.

Mendelssohn was born in a ghetto in the worst possible conditions and *Haydn* started his life as a singer, lost his voice at the age of 18 and lived a miserable existence while composing his masterpieces late at night.

The one thing that these artists all had in common was their unwavering belief in themselves and their professional skills. Ultimately, their integrity towards their work gave them fame and fortune. We, like them, must not be put off by disappointments. When people of character have their backs to the wall, they fight. Every one of us is an artist in his own way and has experienced difficult times. Creating a beautiful painting, a symphony or doing the work that we do is very similar. It requires the same dedication, the same integrity, the same enthusiasm and the same creativity. So let's get on with it.

IT'S UP TO YOU

My talk can be summed up by the story of an old man whom they called the Oracle, because of his visionary powers. Two young boys from the local village had heard of the Oracle's genius and decided to test his wisdom. One day they went into a field to catch a butterfly, holding it between his hands the one boy said to the other, "We will ask him what I have in my hands and being so intelligent, he will answer, 'it's a butterfly'. Then we will ask him if it is alive or is dead. If he answers 'alive' I will squeeze gently until it's dead, and if he says dead, I will open my hands and let it fly away. In this way, we can prove him wrong and expose his so-called visionary powers".

With this plan, they went to the Oracle and one boy asked him, "What have I got in my hands?"
The alert eye of the old man had already seen a piece of the butterfly's wing sticking out of the boy's hands and answered, "A butterfly!"
"Is he alive or is he dead?" asked the boys.
"The answer to that question," replied the Oracle, "... lies in your hands!"

In a similar way, the success or failure of your enterprise, lies in your hands.

MOTIVATIONAL

In closing, ladies and gentlemen, David did not become great when he slew Goliath, but at the moment he decided to try. Within each one of us there is that seed of greatness. All that is needed is a good storm to bring the raindrops that will become the catalyst for it to grow.

If Thomas Edison had gone to business school, we would all still be reading by candlelight. You must ride on ahead of human interests. The surfer on the inside of a great wave, is like the on-rushing swell of enthusiasm that greets a timely idea. Get in front of that force and ride the wave all the way to a successful landing.

The secret is to find something positive in everything that happens, and keep right on going. It's not how hard you fall that counts ... but how high you bounce back! I would rather be on the side of a man who has lost and came back fighting, than be on the side of a man who has only known victory.

BIG BUSINESS IS SMALL BUSINESS WITH AN EXTRA NOUGHT

The small business is the backbone of our society. Find something you like doing best and you will soon find someone who is prepared to pay you to do it for them. Shortly after the great depression, a clergyman in the little Eastern Cape town of Molteno, recognised that the hardship was continuing. He called a meeting at his parish in the Dutch Reformed Church and preached to the women of his congregation from the parable of the talents. After the service he gave each one of them ten cents as a talent from God. Before returning home, ouma Greyvenstein spent her ten cents on ingredients for making rusks. She was good at baking rusks and had developed her own recipe. Back on the farm she baked the rusks, took them back to Molteno where she sold them to visiting farmers' wives. Within days she was receiving floods of orders and soon she was established in a small business. Today on the farm Friedenheim her factory still stands where she employs 300 people who make OUMA rusks for the market.

By the 1950's, the capital reserves from OUMA's factory had increased to the point where diversification was necessary so she sent her three sons to foreign food fairs to look for ideas.

Her talents had increased substantially. Her son, Leon, came back with an idea he had seen in Germany, making potato chips from good quality potatoes. He wanted to use the name LION from his own name, Leon, for this new product but it was already controlled by other interests, so he used the Swahili translation Simba Chips.

By the late 1980's, the group had shown a compound growth of 28,6 % annually and turnover stood at R237 million. From only ten cents a food empire had grown.

A TREE BEARING FRUIT

I close my talk, ladies and gentlemen, with the ingredients for making a good product. Perhaps it is only necessary to look at a tree bearing fruit. There can be few sights more beautiful. With its branches hanging under the weight of its peaches, what a sight it is! Have you ever thought of it? To get that tree to produce, requires many things. It must be subjected to the right amount of wind, a certain amount of frost, the correct dosage of sunlight and sufficient rain. It must also be pruned and sprayed before it can deliver its best. Too much sunshine or too little rain, too much frost or too much wind, or not enough pruning or spraying too late, could end up in a poor result and, so you see that, once again the difference between success and failure is often very small, so much so that it is difficult to measure. Knowledge is, of course, very important, you must know what to do or when and how to do it.

HUMOROUS CLOSE

Well, after so many marvellous speakers, it makes it very difficult to round off the final session of this wonderful day, leaving you motivated and raring to go! My predicament reminds me of the elephant and snake who decided to have a game of snooker in the bush.

Elephant: But we don't have any balls, table or cue, how on earth can we play snooker?

Snake (very motivated): Let's make up a few of our own rules. We don't need a table, balls or a cue! Just look here!

Snake puts the end of his tail in his mouth, forms a hoop like a bicycle wheel and wheels himself around and around Elephant.

Snake: Come on, this could count for a red and yellow.

Elephant agrees to Snake's innovative rules and lifts himself onto his front legs, walking around balancing only on his front feet.

Snake: Okay, I'll give you a red and a yellow for that as well.

Snake corkscrews his way through a bale of hay, demanding that he gets at least a red and a pink for that one.

Elephant matches this by doing a ballet dance and so the two of them carry on, matching each other's performances for a couple of hours until eventually, quite exhausted, they sit down and say simultaneously: How on earth can anyone win in this game?

Snake: I'll tell you what, I'll wriggle up through your trunk all the way through your body and out the other end.

Elephant: Well, if you can do that, I think you win.

Snake darts off into the elephant's trunk, through his body and just then, Elephant sticks his trunk up his own you-know-what and says: How's that for a snooker?!

Well, you must be wondering how I am going to snooker all the brilliant speakers we have heard today? That would be a formidable task indeed. Fortunately for me, I am not here to snooker them, but to thank them.

GET YOURSELF STEAMED UP

Imagine a locomotive steaming across the countryside with its heavy load to pull. How does this absolute miracle of power and motion steaming along endlessly manage? Well, the answer is simple, inside that locomotive there is a little man who stokes up the fire and that fire gets the water to boil and that boiling water builds up a head of steam that gets the engine moving – and it becomes motivated. The interesting part is that lukewarm water doesn't take a locomotive anywhere, and neither will lukewarm enthusiasm lift a person to any level of achievement. Yet, the difference between lukewarm and boiling is really very small, with the same amount of preparation and the same amount of effort, the stoker starts a fire in that engine, but if he quits stoking that fire before it comes to the boil, nothing happens.

Similarly, the difference between success and failure is so small that no one can really tell where one ends and the other begins. Just when one man gives up because life has dealt him an uppercut, the other, who has had as many defeats and as many blows below the belt, and who has less genius into the bargain, goes on to ultimate achievement. Simply because he comes back and he tries again, never giving up. So it is, that when you stop trying you become lukewarm. It's like going fishing without any bait. The chances of your catching anything is so remote that you are just wasting your time. You might as well wink at a pretty girl in the dark – she will never get the message.

EDUCATION AND PLANNING

To be effective in any job, you must acquire knowledge in order to educate yourself for the job you are doing. That is of course, if you want to do it properly. It is no good just being a positive thinker and believing that you can whip the pants off a heavyweight in the boxing ring. You must also know that if you get into that ring and you are not physically prepared, he is going to knock your block off. You must realise that if a man starts off on a train journey from Johannesburg to Cape Town and he only buys a ticket to Beaufort West, there is something wrong with his planning.

Being motivated is great, but you must understand your constraints. It is different if you get sidetracked for a while or the wind blows you off course, or the weather forces you to land at a different destination, but that does not mean that you have reached the end of your journey. This was illustrated to me quite vividly when some months ago, I was on my way to Windhoek and for the first time in 25 years, the plane couldn't land because of mist. We were informed by the captain that we were going to land at Keetmanshoop, 500 km from our destination. The captain dealt with the problem admirably. He had many thousands of hours of flying education, practice and training. There was no stress, worry or concern on the faces of the passengers. His voice came over the loudspeaker system full of confidence. He said, "Ladies and gentlemen, we regret that due to poor visibility, we are unable to land at Windhoek Airport and for your own safety, we are going to deviate to Keetmanshoop where we will wait until the mist clears". A few hours later, after an interesting visit to Keetmanshoop, we were in Windhoek.

The point is this : that captain had probably flown from Johannesburg to Windhoek a few hundred times before, but it was 25 years since a plane had not been able to land at Windhoek because of mist. This pilot didn't abandon or abort his journey, he was indeed taken off course for a while, but thanks to his training he got us back on track again. In our jobs, things don't always work out the way we plan. There are sometimes detours. My message today is: don't quit, don't give up – no one is beaten until he gives up, and remember that things always seem to be at their darkest just before the sun comes up and a new day begins! But that new dawn will be so much greater with some sensible planning.

YOU CAN IF YOU THINK YOU CAN

A lowveld farmer found a lion cub in the bush one day and took it home with him. Soon the lion became quite domesticated. As it grew to maturity the farmer derived a lot of pleasure from scaring the wits out of his visitors by leaving them alone in his lounge, while supposedly fetching drinks, and letting his full-grown lion walk nonchalantly into the room.

His pleasure ended when one day his wife came racing towards him in a bakkie through the veld to declare that the lion had got into the sheep kraal and was killing all their sheep. Without hesitation, he took a whip from behind the seat of his bakkie and rushed to the kraal. Upon arrival, he gave the lion a merciless whipping. The lion was particularly ferocious that day, clawing, snarling and even attempting to bite the farmer. The farmer didn't give an inch. He whipped the lion so soundly that he eventually withdrew to the shade of a marula tree where he lay licking his wounds. The farmer and his wife then retired to their home for a cup of coffee. You can imagine their surprise when they arrived home to find their tame lion sleeping on the lounge carpet.

Amazingly, while the farmer thought that it was his tame lion, he was capable of whipping him. His attitude convinced him that he could and he did. One wonders what would have happened if he had suddenly realised that it was a wild lion.

YOU CAN'T IF YOU THINK YOU CAN'T

Have you ever been to a circus and seen a full-grown elephant chained to a silly little peg in the ground. What a ridiculous sight! With his strength he could pull the peg from the ground or snap the chain that holds him prisoner and walk away to be free forever, but he doesn't. Well, why doesn't he? The answer is that ever since he was a tiny little elephant, he has been chained to that peg. As a baby he tried desperately to free himself without success. Eventually he became conditioned to believe that, when that chain was fixed around his leg and attached to the peg, he could not move away.

In much the same way, we are conditioned to believe that we cannot break away from tradition. Today, you can snap that chain, pull out the peg that holds you prisoner and walk into a new life.

WHAT MOTIVATES YOU?

I am motivated by stories of success, love and beauty. I find that if there is just a small glowing ember in my heart, it becomes a raging furnace when stoked with stories of people who have experienced success.

Have a good look at the next motivated person you see. Notice how their eyes glint, see the brisk gait in their stride. Admire their smile, feel the power in their handshake and witness their enthusiasm for life. A living dynamo, a source of nuclear energy, they have discovered the secret of success. Let me share it with you: you cannot make a fire with dead embers, but if you have a little spark left, fuel it! Fuel it with your dreams, hopes and desires. Adopt the right attitude and support it with all the thrust you have. Focus on the positive things that are happening around you.

When Roger Bannister became the first man on earth to smash the four minute barrier in the mile in 1954, he said he knew that, physically, he was strong enough to do it. It remained for him to convince himself mentally that he could.

Bannister's removal of the four minute barrier motivated others to follow suit. His time of three minutes 59,4 seconds has since become commonplace. In a similar way to an athlete becoming fit to perform on the track, we can become work fit. The harder we work, the more fit we become. The old adage, *if you want something done, ask a busy man*, has its foundation in being work fit.

AGRICULTURAL SOCIETY

A speaker at a recent agricultural congress explained how a cleric's collar can lead to some rather irreverent confusion. Van gets on a train and sees a man wearing his collar back to front. Gentleman that he is, he waits a while before asking the reason for this odd custom.
"I am a Father," comes the reply.
"That's funny. So am I," says Van, "but I wear my collar normally."
"Yes," explains the parson patiently, "but you see, I am the Father of many."
Van remains nonplussed. "I have 12 children, but I have never worn my collar like yours."
"Well, I am actually the Father of 2 000," elaborates the parson.
A little indignant by this stage, Van's brusque retort is, "I think you should wear your pants back to front, not your collar."

CHAPTER THREE

SAMPLE SPEECHES

CHAPTER THREE

SAMPLE SPEECHES

STANDING OVATION

A few years ago I was invited to give a motivational talk in Cape Town. The theme of the convention was Good Hope. It was well-chosen because our economy had advanced from the one disaster to the next miracle. Successive ministers of finance were too political in their approach to solve any of our country's problems. They were financing unachievable political ideals and an escalating war on our borders. This was just a minor part of it. Sanctions, embargoes and boycotts made things very difficult to survive in business. High interest rates, high taxation, high inflation, high unemployment, high government spending and low confidence were the order of the day. All the danger signs were flashing – what about our country's enormous foreign debt? I accepted the invitation before I realised what I was doing. The organisers had also invited a top American speaker to add a little fire and brimstone to the occasion in the hope of attracting more paying delegates to make the convention fly.

Well, you can imagine my problem, I had to project a good hope message while it seemed that the only hope was no hope at all. I thought that maybe I could find a university professor at one of our faculties of commerce who could identify a few positive aspects in our economy and share them with me. South Africa's business men and women, I thought, are the most versatile in the world. To survive this total onslaught, they must also be the best!

Reading the *Business Times* one Sunday morning, the top 100 businessmen of the year were featured together with a photograph, the companies they represented and their achievements. I thought to myself, now here was a great reservoir of knowledge, experience and expertise, if only I could source that for information.

On the day when I had to stand and deliver, this is what I said:
Ladies and gentlemen, as you are all real estate practitioners, I would like to share with you a poem by an anonymous author, which you may find appropriate.

A man knocked at the Pearly Gates
His face was scarred and old
He stood before the man of fate
For admission to the fold
What have you done, St Peter asked,
To gain admission here?
I've been in property, Sir, he said
For many and many a year
The Pearly Gates swung open wide
St Peter touched the bell
Come in and choose your harp, he said
You've had your share of hell!

In preparing this *Good Hope* talk here is what I did. First of all, I wrote a letter to every university in South Africa and asked their respective professors in economy to give me a positive forecast for the next 12 months so that we might all go home from this convention fired with *Good Hope*. Secondly, I wrote to a number of top South African men and women, all of whom have had a successful business career spanning many peaks and valleys and I asked them to give us a message that would inspire us to carry on regardless of the state of our economy.

I must admit that I had hoped for a more encouraging reply to the first part of my plan, but it nevertheless revealed the reality of our problems and I dealt with those replies as follows:

University of Stellenbosch
Your letter puts me in an unenviable position because I just find it impossible to be optimistic about the next 12 months. Frankly, I feel that one should be careful

not to create a feeling of false optimism because the result may cause a lack of optimism for the 12 months or even longer, thereafter. What I want to say is that painful adjustments will have to be made in the coming months in the interest of greater prosperity in future.
C.L. McCARTHY

Potchefstroom University
I am definitely not pessimistic about long-term expectations in the South African economy but for the next 12 months I certainly cannot be optimistic either.
D.P. ERASMUS

University of Durban-Westville
At the moment all short-term indicators do not reflect optimism for the next 12 months. Provided tight monetary and fiscal policies are introduced and maintained, it is possible that the economy will be set for growth in two years time.

The property market, especially housing, might still decline a further 15 % over this time period. Two years down the line housing prices are likely to accelerate and thereafter increase at least at the level of inflation.
PROF. A.J. ARKIN

University of South Africa
I am not optimistic about possible improvements in the economy over the next 12 months. Furthermore, I doubt whether you will find any optimists among the economists at present.
PROF. J.A. DÖCKEL

University of the Witwatersrand
The Reserve Bank's policy of high interest rates is absolutely wrong. My views on this matter are contained in the December edition of Barclays Business Brief.
PROF. D.J.J. BOTHA

Here is an extract from his article which appeared just after the interest rates eased a little. I quote: *The reduction in the prime overdraft rate which has now occurred will at least help to reduce costs in manufacturing and in the economy generally, although it is probably true to say that the entire interest rate structure will have to come down much more if the threat of overkill still hanging over the economy is to be removed. Indeed, it could be argued that the increase in the prime overdraft rate from 22% to 25 %, together with the tightening of the hire purchase credit terms, came at a time when the economy was already slowing down quite appreciably in response to the earlier rise in interest rates, as well as the GST and company tax increases imposed earlier on and which were then starting to make their impact felt on both corporate and personal spending decisions. The measures were accordingly unnecessary and probably merely inflicted undue damage to business and to employment. The reduction in prime which has now been made thus merely starts to correct a policy imbalance and to relieve some of the undue pressure imposed on the economy.*

University of Natal
I fear that at this moment I am not really in a position to help you. I have posted your letter on the staff notice board, asking anyone in the department who may wish to communicate with you to do so directly.
PROF. G.J. TROTTER

Anonymous, probably a student, sent this letter: *All this fuss about the economy for delegates at your Good Hope convention. Just tell them that estate agents create their own economy, as the following true story will illustrate:*

An estate agent booked into the hotel at Matubatuba. He gave the reception a R50 holding deposit to make sure that he had a place to sleep after his hard day's work. The hotel proprietor was delighted with his windfall – he hadn't had a guest for more than a week! He immediately went across the road to the butcher and paid R50 off on his long overdue account. The butcher paid the chemist who paid the grocer who then paid the doctor for services rendered many months before. The doctor had already received a summons for not paying his account at the hotel off-sales, so he quickly went to settle up and as he handed the R50 to the hotel proprietor in payment of his debt ... the estate agent walked in again and explained that the high interest rates impacted so negatively on his business that it caused him to have a re-think and that he would be wasting his time and money if he spent the night. He soon negotiated the cancellation of his booking and with his R50 back in his pocket, drove back to Durban. The point you must make to your convention

CHAPTER THREE

delegates is that even though the agent made no sales at all, his visit resulted in everybody else in the town being paid! So please urge the delegates to keep trying because even when they don't succeed they are a vital link in our economy.

This brings me to the second part of my address to this convention – the part that has *given me* Good Hope for the future of South Africa and all its people.

Looking at big business, we find that we have a reservoir of wealth and knowledge that has withstood the test of time and I am delighted that I have been able to extract from some of our top people their personal experiences. I have a message so powerful to give you today that even if this was the only lecture you attended during this entire convention, it would be worth the trouble and the expense that you went to be here. I wrote a letter to each of the top 100 businessmen asking them to allow us to be privy to their lives and experiences, so that we may all see what it takes to stay at the top! Sadly, they are not here personally to deliver their messages to you this morning and I have had to decide what to use from the many letters received. When I read them to you and their lives unfold before you, I want you to see if you can recognise them, now hear this:

1. *The Good Hope convention should not only attempt to search for practical proposals in order to build confidence for future progress, but also to establish a modus operandi for the multi-social demographic concentration of people who must live out their lives in our rapidly changing environment.*

   For no matter what time you rise you cannot hasten the dawn and once that dawn has come you cannot reverse the light of day. If we are like patients in the intensive care unit, then it is too late to take two aspirins and a laxative! It won't help us anymore – what we really need is a completely new treatment. Everyone in this audience has a vital role to play and a contribution to make. We must change our attitudes; change is like the common cold – it spreads with great rapidity!
   C.J. SAUNDERS

33

2. *I have given your request a lot of thought and feel that I can best help you by sending you the following:*

   You are already very distressed about the economy, and therefore I do not wish to add to your misery. But these issues do to some extent establish a mutual bond amongst us. In the search for solutions in each of the problems, there is the golden thread of this mutual bond. A need for a mental frame of mind which is essential when facing up to the many challenges confronting us.

   What do we, as ordinary human beings, need in order to turn problems irrespective of their nature into opportunities? We need faith, wisdom, insight and sound judgement. In the environment in which we live, the real danger is not that computers will begin to think like men, but that men will begin to think like computers.

   ### Faith
   To me personally this is the most powerful driving force. Faith in a creator mightier than ourselves gives direction, momentum and a sense of responsibility to our existence. It elevates us to a level of moral values constituting the essence of our human existence and enabling us to maintain sound human relations.

   But above all, it is the basis of an optimistic world and life view – the ability to sing songs of hope for a new day while in the dark of night.

   ### Wisdom
   Wisdom is to have the appropriate knowledge for a specific set of circumstances at a given point in time. But it also includes the right frame of mind. Intelligence and spiritual attitude go hand in hand in the exercise of wisdom.

   Under circumstances where the individual is severely tried and tested in his ability to perform adequately, it is essential that the totality of our individual existence be emphasised. That requires wisdom in our thinking, in our action and in our communication with family, colleagues and subordinates.

Insight
Our situation cries for solutions. To find answers – not only on survival for the present – but also on interpreting the future, preparing ourselves for opportunities which are bound to come our way. It will demand study and preparation. It requires a lot of thinking. Make time to think. It is essential that we create adequate opportunity to sit back and think. To develop insight, but also to dream dreams.

Judgement
The ability to judge soundly is essential in planning our future and improving on our past performance. Sound judgement is a prerequisite to achieve optimum utilisation of people and natural assets. The imperative is greater than ever to put all our cards on the table and critically assess our situation.

It is very tempting in times of a severe downturn to throw everything overboard and to run away from our responsibilities. May I remind you that it is not life that matters in the first instance, but the courage you bring to it.

Leadership
The quality of our leadership is at present being severely tried. Insofar as it indicates the extent of a depression, present conditions are the worst in our post-war history. Our economy has crumbled and our companies are suffering serious losses, not only as a result of market conditions but also of exchange and interest rate difficulties.

You, and your families, are being subjected to severe stresses and strains and I have much sympathy and understanding for you.

May I appeal to you not to allow yourselves to be overcome by that which is negative, but to believe in a better future which the process of change will bring about. Success never remains absent from those who dream, think and talk success. As Paul Getty said: ...there is no end to success.
C.J.F. HUMAN

It is essential that we create adequate opportunity to sit back and think. To develop insight, but also to dream dreams.

Success never remains absent from those who dream.

As succinctly put by Rudyard Kipling:
If you can dream and not make dreams your master,
if you can think and not make thoughts your aim,
if you can meet with triumph and disaster
and treat those two imposters just the same,

...he goes on to say ...*the world is yours*
and what's more you'll be a man, my son.

3. *For my part, I can only say that I have always believed in what I set out for. In order to achieve one's economic goals one should not allow oneself to be too influenced by media reports because the gloom of today could be the boom of next month and vice versa. The long-term economic trend in South Africa must of necessity be upward.*
   DR F.J.C CRONJE

4. *The conditions for a successful career in my opinion, is to have an above-average common sense, the ability to lead people, be motivated and be able to persevere. The times in which that we are living demand a strong dose of driving force and endurance. Our motto should be: VASBYT!*
   DR F.J. DU PLESSIS

5. *All of us have had career setbacks at some stage or other and I am no exception. When I was about 40 and progressing well in my career, the group of companies of which I was then director, was the subject of a take-over. While it initially looked as if it would be to my benefit, it became obvious, pretty quickly, that the human values of the new personalities were such that one could not live with them. At the time it seemed to me that the high hopes that I had of building a big career had been frustrated and that in fact my career was at an end. I had to change jobs and accept a lesser position in a smaller organisation.*

   Realising that there were forces in my life which were beyond me and my control, I decided quite consciously that I had better attend to the things that I could control, get my head down and do the job at hand as effectively as

CHAPTER THREE

possible. I did just that and within two years doors began to open and opportunities presented themselves far beyond my then expectations.

From that, comes two lessons for me. Firstly, that you had better attend to the areas of activity under your control and not concern yourself with what is beyond your control. Do the job at hand well, do your best this day and at times in your life when things start going badly, just keep your head down.

Secondly, one's fastest and deepest learning comes during periods of adversity. It is when things go wrong that one learns the most and in that process one develops intuition and sensitivity. I do not believe that one does much character and personality development lying in the sun on the beach.
J. MAREE

6. Let me say that my father lost his job in the early 1930's as a result of the great depression. The family survival kit was to go down to a very small village in the eastern Cape, called Molteno and to remain there until 1937, by which time I was nine years old. The area in which we lived, in addition to suffering the pains of the great recession itself, also went through some three years of drought, two years of locust swarms and then finally, one year of flood which resulted in the majority of farmers (other than the very wealthy) going bankrupt. We then returned to Port Elizabeth – the town in which I was born – and continued to live in difficult circumstances through to the outbreak of World War II. I do not want to give you the impression that we were amongst the most unfortunate because that would not be true. However, one of the tasks that I was allocated each month, was to go and talk to the butcher, the grocer and the outfitter and to persuade them to let us pay only that portion of their monthly account which we could afford. From this, you will realise that we were pretty well permanently in difficulty and debt.

The net result of this experience was that when I first began to work, in 1946, I had an overriding ambition to become as near indispensable as possible, in the shortest possible time. I consistently set annual targets to achieve promotion and in my early thirties first set my sights on the prospect of *becoming a director of a company for which I worked. By my mid-thirties, I had achieved the position of managing director, with all my colleagues on the board being considerably older than I was.*

As an aside, it is perhaps worth mentioning that I was a very sickly child and spent probably more than one third of my life in bed, up to the age of about fourteen.

All I am trying to demonstrate with this little story is that I believe adversity can eventually create a driving force in people and that this adversity does not have to be any one single trauma, but can just as well be a longish history, which first creates the desire to achieve security but later creates the desire to be highly successful.

Finally, I believe that too many businessmen make the mistake of believing that they are in 'The Real Estate Business' or 'The Motor Business' or 'The Travel Business'. The first group should understand that they are in the business of helping people to achieve their dreams of comfort and security; the second should understand that they are in the business of solving transportation problems of large companies and matching the dreams and aspirations of private people; the third should understand that they are in the business of opening windows to new worlds of adventure and excitement.
C. ADCOCK

Is it any wonder that Toyota leads the field during one of the most serious recessions that the motor industry has ever experienced?

Leaders are not born! I have never heard of a doctor announcing that he had just delivered a new leader! I have never seen a newspaper announcement stating that a new leader was born today! Have you? It's sometimes only when things go wrong that we come right!

Too many little boys and girls set off brashly after breakfast to roam the world only to come home, humbled and hungry at dinnertime.

But please listen to this, here is another gem:

CHAPTER THREE

7. *Thank you for your letter. I am not normally inclined towards telling others about my misfortune – on the contrary, I believe that while adversity is never pleasant, it is nevertheless a necessary ingredient for success, so I will share a few of my thoughts with you.*

God was good to me and blessed me with the most wonderful parents. They influenced my attitude to life in a positive way and taught me that adversity was always negated by the challenge it created.

I was just a little girl when Sharpeville occurred and my father had just sunk the family savings into a small property which we developed into accommodation for a few neighbourhood shops. He couldn't find tenants in those dark days and the interest rate working on the mortgage bond seemed to eat up all our capital. I will always remember my mother's attitude as she encouraged my father by saying, "Don't worry, darling, we still have each other!"

We were not a jet-set family by any manner of means, but knew the power of using those small wonderful words in life, like God, love, wife, home. I heard them often and will always be grateful to my parents for leaving me this heritage. They gave me faith, confidence, persistence and stability.

I have learnt to turn my weaknesses into strengths and in the absence of adversity, will create my own challenge as I set higher and higher goals. It's like someone throwing down the gauntlet and is part of my success formula.

You can tell the delegates at your Good Hope convention from me that they must have faith and be prepared to pay the price of commitment and persistence in the face of adversity if they want to succeed ... As a man thinketh, so he is. The right attitude is all that is needed. One of my greatest triumphs in life is to achieve success through building up other people, people who think that they are broken down because: I'm black; I'm broke; I'm uneducated or I'm a woman. For me, the best reward is to reveal to them whence they have come or where they are going is not important. What is crucial is to discover that greatest of all gifts ... the potential which is inside all of us, what comes from within us. This is my first priority in life and I love doing it. I thrive on challenges. I inevitably create my own because they are evidence that I am alive and working and I thank God for giving me the courage to overcome those challenges so that I can continually set even higher goals.

In conclusion, my philosophy is a simple one: You can! If you believe you can. One of my favourite sayings is: He who attempts the impossible, has little competition.
REEVA FORMAN

Did you feel the power in this message? Here again you find that attitude alone is not enough, it must be supported by full thrust! A jumbo jet moving along a runway in a take-off attitude will not leave the ground unless the captain pushes the throttle into the full power position.

But, ladies and gentlemen, here is a reply that I shall cherish for as long as I live, simply because of its determination and beauty.

8. *Your letter dealing with your proposed address to the Good Hope convention refers. I reply in the hope that by relating my story, perhaps someone in your audience may be encouraged to be more fearless in the face of obstacles along the way.*

   I was four years old when the great depression of 1933 impoverished our nation. My father and mother had six children and were very poor. We were lucky though – Dad had a job. He was a conductor on the railways in Kimberley and could feed us. During the war, an accident on the job put him out of action for so long that sick-pay ceased to provide an income for the family, so I had to find a job and I left school after Standard Seven to help. The railways were good to me – they employed me as a labourer ... I fetched and carried the tools for an artisan. After the war the soldiers came home and were given all the good jobs. Soon afterwards, I was accidentally hit on the jaw with a four pound hammer and fell to the ground from the top of a steam locomotive. I was told that I was too light for the job.

   I used to daydream a lot and still do and believe that it's necessary for all of us to daydream now and then. I suppose it's because I truly believe that one can achieve anything that your mind can conceive. Success or failure is entirely up to oneself.

CHAPTER THREE

By now my father was earning money again and I decided on more education, so I went back to school. This time I made it to Standard Eight and thereafter got a job, first as a postman and then with a gents' outfitter shop in Kimberley. After a short while I rejoined the railways because they paid more. I was now earning £9 per month as a messenger boy and saving a little. During that year, I attended the Northern Cape Technical College (not with matriculation exemption). I passed the railway's clerical tests and was selected from 300 candidates for transfer to the South African Airways. In those days there was no Johannesburg International Airport – we operated from Rand Airport in Germiston as the head office of S.A.A. I learnt part time to fly tiger moths and other light aircraft and to this day have retained my interest in flying.

A burning desire for further education gripped me once more, but without matriculation to my credit I could not obtain a university entrance without at least matric exemption. The South African Airways gave me unpaid study leave to enable me to go back to school. Diamantveld Hoërskool in Kimberley admitted me as a pupil on condition that I shaved off my moustache! I got my university pass after six months of school, but it required a disciplined approach. My years with the railways had taught many wonderful lessons, not the least of which was the three-shift per day method of working. Every eight hours a new shift would come on duty to keep the railroad running. I soon learnt that the railways required my labour for eight hours a day; my body needed an eight hour shift for resting; but there was the magic and great challenge of the third shift that was to be the key to my future – if I wasted it I would probably soon be back to being a messenger for the railways, but if I used it constructively, it would greatly enhance the quality of my future life.

I accepted the challenge and was admitted to the University of the O.F.S. I had £3 in my pocket and had chosen a B.Sc. degree because then it was the in-thing to study science. Two years later, because of being colour blind, I had to abandon this career while the university instructed their attorneys to take legal action against me for the recovery of class and hostel fees that I was unable to pay. While studying during the day, I worked at night in a local hotel where I worked on their switchboard and did other chores and also utilised the remaining time during my 'third shift' working at a local library in Bloemfontein. In order to pay off my study debt, I had to 'milk' the poisonous venom from snakes and together these two jobs paid £10 per month. I eventually graduated with a BA. LLB. Degree, studying part time.

In 1961, I was admitted as an advocate to the high court of the British Protectorates – Lesotho, Swaziland and Botswana, while also practising in South Africa. In 1962, I accepted an appointment as senior lecturer in law at a university in Natal. It was during this period that I became interested in labour law and I soon found myself working in Germany, in various cities, where I studied their labour laws intensively and I was eventually able to relate the British and European laws to our own. My thesis for my doctoral degree was on boycotts. In 1966, I was appointed professor of commercial law at the University of Port Elizabeth and since then I have enjoyed being appointed to various other highly responsible positions, including being asked to be personal advisor to the Minister of Labour.

Reflecting on my life and progress, you can tell your delegates at your convention that I took strength from great authors from the past and used their writings as a yardstick and as inspiration for my own life: Shakespeare said, 'Every man is a universe unto himself'. I see this as meaning that every man is a living dynamo – a source of nuclear energy – he must just discover his own detonator. Cicero said, 'To live a decent life even if only for a short period, is long enough'.

I am particularly grateful to four areas of my life that have given me stimulus and direction. They are:
1. *I am grateful for the mistakes I have made, for they have taught me the most;*
2. *I am grateful for all the trials and tribulations that I have experienced, for they have built my character and personality and made me the man I am;*
3. *I am grateful for all my critics, for they have kept me humble;*
4. *I am grateful for all my enemies, since it is amongst them that you have to keep your head high. Psalm 27:6 sums it up: "And now shall mine head be lifted up above mine enemies round about me: therefore will I offer in his tabernacle sacrifices of joy; I will sing yea, I will sing praises unto the Lord."*

CHAPTER THREE

In conclusion, you may tell your delegates that dedication to their cause, involvement in their work, their environment and their institute are important factors, but that all-important challenge and magic of the 'third shift' is what makes the difference. Opportunity does not knock at your door, you must prepare yourself to recognise it when it passes so that you too can benefit from it. Success or failure is entirely up to you.
PROF. N. WIEHAHN

He adds, "I used to daydream a lot and still do, and I believe that it is necessary for all of us to daydream now and then ..."

Colin Adcock says, "... we must help them to achieve those dreams."

C.J.F. Human says, "We must develop insight, but also dream dreams. Success never remains absent from those who dream."

A famous line of poetry reads: *Hold fast to dreams, for if dreams die, life is a broken-winged bird that cannot fly.* For too many people, life has become a dreamless, monotonous, boring routine that they can't take pride in anymore. We have to learn to: dream – study – plan – take action. Put shoulder to the wheel – but remember to push. Dr Anton Rupert is one of my heroes. Regrettably, on the eve of my letter arriving, he departed on an extensive overseas visit and did not have time to reply. He did, however, send me a copy of his latest book, called *Priorities for co-existence* and I would like to quote just a few passages from it.

He reminds us, first of all, of our country's slogan: "*Unity is strength,*" and goes on to say that "this unity should not be confused with similarity. South Africa's strength lies in its difference – in the richness of variety. Greatness is measured by the ability to think big and to do big things; self-development is the only lasting development. The creative ability of the entrepreneur, the individual who risks his capital to make a profit for himself – this is the driving force of our economy."

Summary

In summing up the following clear guidelines should give *Good Hope*. You are the only one who can use your ability – it is an awesome responsibility, but what a discovery when you find it!

I think that the authors of the letters that we have dealt with today have succeeded in perhaps just lighting a match for us, an experience that we should never forget. It is clear that when people of character have their backs to the wall ... they fight back with great resolve.

We have repeatedly heard the word adversity and were told that:
>Adversity creates a challenge
>
>Adversity creates a driving force
>
>Adversity is never pleasant but it is nevertheless a necessary ingredient for success
>
>One's fastest and deepest learning comes during periods of adversity.

The new Oxford Advanced Dictionary of Current English says: *A brave man smiles in the face of adversity.* We must pay the price of commitments and persistence in the face of adversity.

To do this:
> We need the right attitude. Remember the magic and the power of the third shift – we need full power.
>
> We must change our attitude if we want to take off and achieve greater heights.
>
> We need a change in our thinking – change is like the common cold ... it spreads with great rapidity.
>
> We must dream: *As a man thinketh, so he is.*
>
> We must attend to the areas of activity under our control – and avoid concerning ourselves with what is beyond our control.

Be grateful for all the trials and tribulations that we have experienced for they have built our characters. There are so many wonderful lessons in these messages from great and wonderful people today that it is difficult to single out one that we can take with us for inspiration ... so let's apply them all!

After a standing ovation I was swamped by requests for a copy of this talk. In fact years later I still get calls asking me for copies. Many of them from people who never even attended the convention. The most satisfying came from the American speaker who had heard from the delegates of my *Good Hope* message and regretted not being present, he desperately wanted a copy as well.

Another standing ovation was in Durban. I had been to Durban and their Drakensberg Mountain conventions many times. KwaZulu Natal always gives a speaker a wonderful welcome. They seem to understand the problems that we face and are closer to a solution for our young democracy than the rest of our country. Their audiences are also more representative of the three great continents of the world, Asia, Europe and Africa, whose people have settled here.

The material for this talk was researched in libraries and by talking to people, politicians and the man in the street. It has two parts to it as the title will show, which made it interesting because the *motivational* part was separate from *a time for change,* yet I was able to merge the two parts into a single talk.

MOTIVATION AND A TIME FOR CHANGE

Ladies and gentlemen, I congratulate your committee on their choice of a theme – *Motivation and a time for change.* There is no better time in our history than right now to be motivated when there is so much happening around us that inspires us. The question most frequently put to me is, how does one stay motivated? Well, I suppose in a way it is like sex, it's a very personal thing, I can't do it for you and you can't do it for me. But wow! What a pleasure! It's like walking into a great field of luscious ripe strawberries, but you only have a small basket. To be motivated is to have the ability to accept a challenge and influence life in a positive way. It's being able to get things done. It is an honest and enduring desire to improve oneself and the people with whom you come into contact.

It is not like the old man who used to sit in church every Sunday and shout, "Use me Lord, use me Lord!" One day the minister thought that he should use this motivated man for the benefit of the entire congregation and so the next week he asked him to paint all the benches. The following Sunday the old man was back in church and while the minister preached, he would shout again but this time a little softer, "Use me, Lord, use me, Lord, but please use me in an advisory capacity".

Motivation is better explained by using the example of the horse race. Just picture for a moment three horses crossing the winning post, the first gets paid R100 000 in prize money, the second R50 000 and the third R10 000. Often the judges need a photo to determine the horse's positions. There is no way that the horse who came first is *ten times* better than the one that comes third and yet he gets *ten times* more money! For only being a fraction better! Let's meet the challenge. Let's be a fraction better from now on, let's get *motivated*.

Don't bother playing noughts and crosses when everyone else around you is playing chess. I am motivated by knowing that there are an awful lot of well-qualified people out there who may take your order before I can get to you, so I have to get moving and in the process give you *better service* as well. Why be average? Develop the energy and spirit of a racehorse and hammer relentlessly at the doors of success until they yield to you. You haven't got it until you get it and when you get it, you must pass it on, because the flame of life is not eternal unless you do pass it on.

Don't be like the people who walk around waiting for their ship to come home. People wishing incessantly they had someone else's ability or talent. Don't become a *prisoner of hope*, you already have the ability you need for

CHAPTER THREE

success. If you remember nothing else I say today, remember this .... *You are not a loser* ... if you *think* that you are a loser, it is only because you *think so*. We must get back to work because work, more than anything else inspires us ... it is *work* which builds great ships, it is *work* that builds bridges and tunnels through mountains. It is *work* that builds our factories, our schools, our hospitals and our highways. By working hard, we develop the ability to do more, in the same way that the athlete runs that extra mile when everyone else is exhausted. Just sitting around wishing, makes no one rich. The good Lord sends the fish, but we must dig for the bait.

Henry Wadsworth Longfellow put it this way:
The heights that great men reached and kept were not obtained by sudden flight,
but those while their companions slept, were toiling upward in the night.

We must become the kind of people that the time in which we are living demands of us. We need strong minds, strong hearts and true grit. We can and must get this country back to work. But we need men and women who can stand before an agitator and damn his treacherous lies. We need people who the spoils of crime cannot buy. We need people with honour, who respect the rule of Law and Justice so that once again we can live without fear and apprehension in this wonderful country of ours. The mistakes and blunders of the past with all the aches and pains that those imperfections brought upon us, must *now, once and for all,* be assigned to history, so that we can live a decent life today and plan a better *tomorrow* for our children and their children's children. The remorse and bitterness for something that happened yesterday, is only kept alive by second rate politicians who keep trying to conceal their own lack of ability.

We must do more than just exist – we must *live*.
We must do more than just touch – we must *feel* for one another.
We must do more than just look – we must *see* the other man's point of view.
We must do more than just hear – we must *listen* to what people are saying and
We must do more than just speak – we must say something *meaningful!*

The clock of life ticks on and our time is running out. We must use our time productively, don't put off for tomorrow that which we can do today. We cannot lose a day nor waste an hour. Don't find yourself in the position of the wife who wrote the following about her husband and the things he didn't do:

Remember the day I borrowed your brand new car and dented it? I thought you'd kill me but you didn't. And the time I dragged you to the beach – and you said it would rain and it did, I thought you'd say 'I told you so' – but you didn't. And the time I flirted with all the guys to make you jealous and you were, I thought you'd leave me – but you didn't.

And do you remember when I spilled that milk on the carpet of your new car, I thought you'd smack me – but you didn't. Yes, there were a lot of things you didn't do, but you put up with me and loved me and protected me. And there were so many things that I wanted to make up to you when you came back from the war but... you didn't.

Don't wait – do it now!

We are privileged to be living in one of the most exciting times in human history, in a country with unlimited opportunities. By being motivated, we can be used for a purpose much greater than ourselves. We must, however, always remember that we are divinely created and armed with a purpose that can make our country succeed. To achieve this, we must recognise that life is a journey not a parking garage. Life is a school, not a cemetery, it is an arena filled with great events that teach, entertain and offers great climaxes. Life is for growth, for movements, for purpose and for achievement. Yesterday is a cancelled cheque, tomorrow a promissory note and today is *cash in hand*. Remember too, that the worst bankruptcy there can possibly be, is the poor soul without enthusiasm. Don't sell yourself too cheap, don't talk yourself down, don't give way to pressure.

CHAPTER THREE

Remember that lovely poem:

Don't bargain with life for a penny,
because life will pay you no more.
However you beg at evening time,
counting your meagre store,
for life is a just employer,
it gives whatever you ask,
but once you have set the waves,
then you must bear the task.
I worked for a menial's hire
only to learn with dismay,
that any wage I'd asked of life
– life would have gladly paid.

We must look forward .... not just at our feet, but towards the horizon if we want to see the dawn of a new day and when that new day comes, we must seize every minute of every hour with courage and conviction because boldness has power, magic and genius in it.

Sometimes we feel despondent, neglected, forgotten, a failure. George Bernard Shaw said:
Nine out of every ten things I ever did were failures. I didn't want to be a failure so I had to work ten times harder.

Even Christ felt despondent, neglected and forgotten. After carrying his cross for a long time and over a great distance he said while hanging on the cross, "My God, my God, why hast thou forsaken me?"

The world is tough out there and yet we can succeed working only half days and it really doesn't matter which 12 hour shift you choose.

Ladies and gentlemen, this brings me to the second part of my talk, a time for change.

There is *pain* and *sorrow* in lives *everywhere*. By understanding this we learn how to share. People may differ in appearance, intelligence and possessions, but our instincts, passions and feelings are very similar. Isolated, a man may be cultured, refined and loving, but in a crowd he becomes a barbarian, he possesses the spontaneity, the violence, the ferocity, enthusiasm and heroism of primitive beings. For example, our Parliament would pass laws and approve other measures collectively, that each of its members would disapprove of on his own, if taken separately. Once the crowd is moving, it is difficult to stem the tide. No man can change the direction of the wind, just as it is difficult to reverse the flow of a river, even over a short distance. We assume that leaders know what they are doing and the fact of the matter is that, in the end, it rests upon the character of those men – that's what really matters, but unfortunately they are a mixture of good and bad.

Sometimes they take us to the brink of disaster and sometimes to oblivion. We found ourselves, not long ago, in a country that was structured like a prison of nations, each language group separate from the other. Sitting on a volcano, ready to erupt. Thank God, common sense prevailed. In this modern world we live in, the socio-economic structures that we have created, such as large shopping centres, have alienated us from one another even more. In earlier times, the water hole was the focal point for friendly discussion, the exchange of information and sharing the ups and downs of human existence. These modern complexes are today's monuments to non-communication. We pass one another by the thousands *alone in the crowd*. With our computers we try to make contact with the world, through pressing a key, but we remain aloof from our fellow human beings and even from ourselves. Our ability to communicate with each other is contained in our ability to share emotions, points of view, aspirations, human experiences, that computer chips cannot provide.

What we need to experience once again is spontaneity, improvisation, quirkiness, an unexpected and unstructured way of dealing with our problems. We must create a climate based on logic to assist us in identifying the most important issues that confront us. We must turn our backs to the past and face a marvellous future, acknowledging the contribution made by all of our people. This great symphony called change must be orchestrated so that all of us will participate in re-inventing our future, identifying our expectations and developing our dreams.

CHAPTER THREE

We must paint our own rainbows but expect a few thunderstorms because they bring the rain. That flash of enthusiasm that ignites the flame of hope and a burning desire within us, to make this country the best place on earth. Nothing lasts forever, things must, do, and will change – forcing us constantly to look at ourselves and ask the questions, who are we, what are we, where have we come from, and most importantly, where are we going?

We are not the only country in the world that is being troubled by the scourge of crime. It is a world-wide phenomenon and it occurs like suicide and madness. When we don't take time to think – take time to work and to love, that is when our dreams start falling apart. Important changes have already been made but we need further positive changes. We must not forget to cure the ills and to release the tension between the haves and the have nots.

We must also accept that no one is born with hatred and prejudice. There is no justification in wanting to impose our will on others. Men should not be judged by their tint of skin, the gods they serve, the vintage they drink, nor by the way they live or sin, but by the quality of their thoughts, their words and deeds. Whenever. I hear people expressing hatred for any race I wonder just what it is within themselves that they hate so much. Because, it is the supply of hatred stored deep inside oneself that causes one to express hatred towards another. To hate is to be evil. Our major problem is clearly one of morality, the first and third world components of our population must penetrate and dismantle the racial divide that keeps us apart. Collectively, we have a responsibility to uphold human dignity and respect for every citizen. We must develop a pride in our nation that will weld us together. Our economy must be kick-started into action so that we can provide employment, food, clothing and shelter for all. I believe that everyone of us is aware of the problems and challenges facing us, but not everyone understands the evolution that is taking place. From now on we are working for South Africa – for all South Africans, regardless of their culture, language and tradition. Wealth is not measured by the amount of gold we have, but by the *talent* and enterprise of our people.

SAMPLE SPEECHES

In closing, I must tell you the story of the balloon salesman who was selling different coloured balloons to children at the Pretoria show grounds. They were all priced the same and one little boy wanted to know, "If I buy a black balloon will it fly as high as the white or pink one?"

"Son," said the salesman, "it is not the colour that makes these balloons fly, it is what's inside them that counts."

The *Good Hope* talk was engineered to last one hour while the *Motivation and a time for change* was for 20 minutes. Your invitation to speak usually decides the length of your talk. The speed with which you deliver, will, to a large extent, determine how much material you should prepare. I find that I require 50% more material than I need to stop on time. It is easier to cut your presentation short and end on time, than to fill in an extra 15 minutes if you run out of speech. I am always impressed with a speaker who speaks without notes. This is the hard way of doing it. I have tried to simulate those speakers and have succeeded, but only when I prepare my talk in the following manner:
1. Write the speech
2. Rehearse it
3. Try to memorise it
4. Use nomenclatures

Put differently, I must experience it, digest it and then deliver it. Using a *nomenclature* is just another way of saying 'I code my speech'. Let me illustrate this by relating a talk I give quite frequently on *marketing*. There are many different components that make up the subject of marketing. One small part deals with a promotional science called public relations. The nomenclature I use for this part of my talk is P.E.N.C.I.L.S. This is briefly how it works:

P *Publications* are an essential tool in the marketing process. If, for example you are selling a product or service that is used by the medical fraternity, you must identify those *publications* that are directed towards your target market and then spend part of your advertising budget with those *publications*. You will also find that editorial copy in those *publications* are welcomed by the editor. Some *publications* allow what is called advertorial. This is simply advertising that appears to be editorial, but the *publication* would charge you for the space that your copy uses, at their advertising rates.

E *Events* are always something to look for. If you could launch your service or product over Easter, Christmas or even a visit by Halley's comet, it gives it a little extra flavour. The opportunities are endless. For example: a promotion to celebrate 21 years in business.

N *News* – North – East – West – South. When last did you have your name in the newspaper – or are you going to wait for the obituary column? Every newspaper editor in the country is looking for news! When something big happens to you, write to the local newspaper editor and tell him about it. You don't have to be a skilled journalist. If he likes your story he will phone and ask you the who – what – when and where bits and write the story in correct journalese himself. But get your name into the newspaper!

C *Community* involvement is an essential part of public relations and it is so easy to get involved. Let us assume that you are launching a new shopping centre in a neighbourhood. You realise that it is important to get the *community* involved. How do you do it? ...It is really quite simple. Contact the chairperson of the local charity or charities. The Cancer Association – The Civilian Blind – The Cripple Care Association – etc., etc. Offer them a small percentage of the turnover on opening day or give them a substantial donation for their cause – provided, of course, they perform some function and are in attendance on the opening day. They could work in the parking lot, collect all the trolleys and return them to their bays, provide refreshments or do light catering for the day. The list is endless. This way you can be sure of their support. Not only will you involve some of the finest workers in the *community* but also most of the respected leaders.

SAMPLE SPEECHES

I   *Identity* media is always an important consideration. Letterheads – calling cards – brochures – newsletters and so on. Not every business is like the jewellery shop with display windows, velvet lined shelves, spotlights and the rest. Your display window is your *identity* media – etc., etc.

L   *Lobbying* has in recent times become very popular. It is an American concept that is beginning to gain significance all over the world. When there is a change of government for instance, you may lose all the political contact you had, overnight. By using lobbyists, you can keep your foot in the door with these representatives. If you have the time or the opportunity to lobby yourself, it could, of course, be more effective. *Lobbying* is the art of getting through to people who would normally not be accessible to you. A *lobby* is also known as a corridor, entrance hall, foyer or passage and by talking to people in these areas you are *lobbying*.

S   *Social* commitment is something all successful enterprises should have. Assuming for a moment that a monument to freedom has been contemplated. The government's hands may be tied. Contributions to fund this monument would have to come from the people. Such a monument cannot be funded by a government or a political party, because if it were, it may represent the feelings of only one sector of the population. It must be a people's monument – a *social* thing which requires everyone to identify with it. If, therefore, a credit card company, for example, had to promote the idea that every time their credit card was used for a purchase, 1% of the value of that purchase would be donated to the freedom monument fund, the problem would be in the process of being solved.

This condensed illustration of using a nomenclature or coding system to remember key words that trigger the rest of your memory into action, is what creates in an audience the feeling of respect, admiration and appreciation. If you want to speak without reading or using cue cards – this is the answer because it prevents the brain from meandering like a stream through a valley. But the basic ingredient is still *practice – practice – practice.*

CHAPTER FOUR

COMMENCEMENT SPEECHES

CHAPTER FOUR

COMMENCEMENT SPEECHES

A MATRIC FAREWELL

Ladies and gentlemen, being with you on this important day is indeed a very special privilege for me, because this is the day that you will commence your lives after completing the initial stages of your education. It is an absolute joy to share this day with you and I congratulate each one of you on achieving your matriculation certificate.

This is an ideal opportunity for me to inspire you to continue with your education, in quest of success and greater wisdom. I suspect, however, that if all the good advice that has been given on these occasions through the years were brought out and put on view today, it would still be as *good as new*. Simply because very little of it has ever been used.

Still, the very nature of this special occasion, provides me with a platform to discuss with you three themes that are important to all South Africans at this time. Firstly, I think that any visitor to this school would be struck by a *sense of tradition*. A tradition that must have developed at this school with its history of more than 100 years. But along with this sense of history and tradition is a second reaction, the compelling atmosphere of *nowness*. Clearly you have learned from the past, but you do not dwell in it. *Your eyes are on today and tomorrow.*

The third idea I would share with you is conveniently provided by the slogan on the Coat of Arms of the Republic of South Africa – '*ex-unitate-vires*' or, unity is strength. Reading the newspapers you may question that, because hardly a day goes by without reading about the dissent amongst political parties and racial groups. What makes the *news*, however, is *only a fraction of the real world*. Television and the daily newspapers chronicle catastrophes, they report on the *doom* and *gloom* aspects of every day life and not on the day-to-day going about our business, that keeps the wheels of life turning.

The same is true of our history books – they catalogue wars, political intrigue, scandals and depressions, but seldom take note of the steady determination and faith reflected in all our people which ultimately enjoyed victory over sometimes insurmountable problems. Today's world may seem to you to be hostile and complex, but there really is nothing new.

South Africa was involved in a war against Great Britain from 1899 to 1902. Thereafter, we fought side by side with Great Britain from 1914 to 1918. We were impoverished by the great depression in the 1930's only to be drawn into the Second World War from 1939 to 1945. We had hardly caught our breath, when from 1948 onwards we entrenched *apartheid*, which became our way of life.

The point I want to make to you today, is that while historians were recording all these disasters, turmoils and tragedies, *great things* were happening, for example, *about 17 years ago – you were born*. And while you were growing up and getting to high school – a new democracy was put into place in South Africa. The doors and windows of friendship and trade opened up all over the world. Tourism is set to take off, with all its opportunities and challenges. Urbanisation has suddenly taken on enormous proportions and four million houses need to be built. This requires the infrastructure to support it, roads, storm water drains, fresh water, electricity, schools, hospitals, universities and much, much more. *You* will be confronted with these challenges and *you* will enjoy the benefits of the solutions.

To inherit a legacy of problems is not so bad. After all, if one generation solved all the problems, what would be left for the next generation to do? Problem solving brings about such good things in life – more answers to cure disease, technological advances, re-kindling of

CHAPTER FOUR

spiritual values, more universal enjoyment of the arts, preservation of our historical treasures, orderly and sensible use of our environment, a whole new *re-birth of love* in a country where a system tore us apart. The greatest satisfaction any of us can have is *solving problems*, whether it is seeking peace and ridding us of the scourge of crime, finding a cure for Aids or success in your chosen career. These problems that everyone has worked on for so long and so hard, will not, however, yield to simple solutions.

To learn to live with the reality that there are *only simple solutions to simple problems* and that complex solutions are sometimes *more complex* than the problems they seek to solve. If that sounds confusing, it may just highlight that one of the greatest problems we face is that of communication. We speak 11 languages all under one roof and sometimes even our home language is misinterpreted. For example: – if your principal had to announce on the public address system, "I have decided to stop streaking on the school grounds", many of you might think that you had missed the show!

Another difficulty is that as a matriculant one has all the answers to all the problems. Each of us is grossly ignorant in some respect. With a matric certificate in your hands, you will know that being grossly ignorant is 144 times worse than ordinary ignorance. As students leaving high school, you are emerging with less ignorance than most. We must not forget, however, that when a student graduates, he ought to be able to *do something*. From what I've learned about this school, you will be very well-equipped to *do things and there is such a lot to do.*

There has never been a time when our country had a greater need for *fresh ideas, the zest you have, the energy of youth.* There has never been a time when all that matters is *what you can do,* not where you come from, the *colour of your skin* or *your gender*. This is the time for equal opportunity. *Your job must be equal to the opportunity.* I must add that opportunity is usually disguised as hard work. But there's no need to be afraid of it. Remember that nothing is really work, unless of course you would rather be doing something else.

COMMENCEMENT SPEECHES

Without exception, all the successful people I know enjoy their work. They approach their jobs as a problem to be solved and they gain their greatest reward and satisfaction *out of arriving at a solution.* It is the sense of accomplishment that really counts, not the financial reward. Remember that money is just a way of keeping score. The same is true of your matric certificate.

Business today is crying out for people who can make things happen, whether it is producing goods, selling them or servicing them! In the professions, there are cures to be found, new technologies to be created and in our country we are desperately looking for new ways to help people reconcile their differences.

Today you will receive our applause for getting through High School. I know you are wise enough, and mature enough to realise that you have not yet *"finished your education."* Life is a continual process of learning, growing, stretching and strengthening your capacity to do, to love and to give, must be further developed. Your matric certificate is like a letter of introduction to the world, a licence to seek opportunity. In business and in the professions, the opportunities are almost overwhelming. The world asks only two things of you – be honest *with yourself* and *with others.*

In closing, let me assure you that here, at this school you have received the tools of useful service and you have been more fortunate than the young man in a story about the Greek teacher, Socrates.

There came to Socrates one day, a rich man's son, named Alcibiades. He asked the way to eternal life. For, to the mind of Socrates, a searcher after knowledge was a searcher after virtue.
Said Alcibiades, "Socrates, how shall I be educated?"
Socrates said: "What can you *do*? Can you drive a mule to the top of the Acropolis, carrying one of those shining blocks of marble to be put on the top of the Parthenon?"
"Oh no", said Alcibiades, "the muleteer does that."
"Can you drive a chariot?"
"Oh no, the charioteer does that."

"Alcibiades, *can you carve a statue?*"
"Oh no, we hire our statues carved."
"Can you cook dinner?"
"Oh no, we have cooks to do that."
"Is it not strange, Alcibiades, that your father should give to his humblest servants a better education than he does his son?" And Alcibiades went away sorrowful, for he loved ease and was slothful.

Your school has taught you *'to do something'*. Whatever you decide to do with your knowledge, *do it with your heart and soul.* Robert Louis Stevenson said, "I know what pleasure is, for I have done good work." Today as we applaud you and say 'good luck' we must also say that the greatest pleasure there is *for doing good work* is the desire and ability to do better work.

COMMENCEMENT ADDRESS

Thank you for the invitation to address the matriculants of your school on this auspicious occasion. Having a child in matric myself this year makes me very much aware of the importance of an occasion like this for all those involved. It is therefore a particular honour to be asked to be a part of it.

Two aspects of occasions like this strike me as remarkable. First, I am always struck by the optimism reflected in having such a function before the last major hurdle of the matriculation examination has actually been cleared. But secondly, I understand the reason of those responsible for the arrangements; they know that nobody would be around for such a function after that event. These two qualities, namely realism and optimism, happen to be the ones about which I wish to share some thoughts with you tonight.

By this time, all of you will be aware that you have reached one of those turning points in life. Leaving school means entering a different world and demands difficult but important choices – whether to enter into university or other post-school training or to follow alternative choices.

Whichever you exercise now, will not only determine what world you will enter, but also much of what your life will be later on. As if all this is not difficult enough, circumstances in South Africa today introduce the choice of whether to seek a future here, or to cut your losses and go elsewhere. You may be excused for even asking, "Is there life after school?"

The South African economy has been in recession for a long time. Although occasionally there are some signs of a modest revival, there is no assurance of ready jobs even for those who qualify in the job market – whether by completing your schooling, university training or a trade. Crime has become almost a normal feature of our daily lives – even if not directly confronted with it, through our awareness. It signifies a rejection of law and order by many of our fellow citizens. In the rest of the world, the topic of discussion as far as South Africa is concerned, no longer appears to be whether our country is a democracy or not but rather how long our youth can be persuaded to remain in the country to help solve its problems.

It would be a miracle if the circumstances prevailing did not leave some scars on us. Indeed, we need to be very realistic in our assessment of how all this is most likely to affect our way of life.

Most certainly we must expect that even with an improvement in the state of our economy, the previously privileged population is not going to have it as good as they were accustomed to. The deficiencies in facilities and services available to rural and sometimes urban people are so huge, especially in comparison with those enjoyed by the privileged that a considerably larger proportion of state expenditure will have to be directed to the needs of the disadvantaged in future. Some are going to have to pay directly for a much larger part of the facilities and services they enjoy. This is already being witnessed by higher school fees, higher tariffs for health services, higher property tax, fewer tax breaks on fringe benefits and other indirect ways of subsidising our high level of living, without a concomitant decrease in the tax burden. We are also going to face more competition in the job market from an increasingly well-trained and experienced black population, while, at the same time, see an increase in the number of rural people coming to live in informal settlements in close proximity to existing residential areas, without the well-ordered conditions that we have become accustomed to. Security conditions will remain tenuous for some years.

These are not pleasant circumstances to contemplate, but in all realism we must face them as facts and those of us who are going to stay in South Africa are going to have to adjust to them. The question is, *"Will it be worth my while?"*

I have little doubt that it will. The very complexity of our society presents many challenges, but the opportunities for creativity in meeting those challenges would be difficult to rival anywhere else in the world.

When I was at school, I sometimes felt that history had cheated me, because all the big and exciting things had already happened – events like the Great Trek and the Anglo Boer War, the discovery of gold and diamonds, the industrial revolution and many more. Little did I know that I would be living through events that are probably the most exciting ever and to which future historians will devote as much and even more attention.

Take only the field in which I am presently engaged, namely, real estate. A few years ago only four million people could buy, sell, occupy and transfer property. Today 40 million people have this privilege. Can you imagine the *demand pull cost push* effect on prices when this economic force starts working its way through? There are so many calls on innovativeness that we can hardly hope to respond to all of them – to find and help put into effect ways in which the productivity and living conditions of tribal farmers in rural areas can be raised, affordable ways in which to improve the housing needs, water, energy and health, requirements of low-income communities, practical ways in which small businesses can be supported towards sustained viability, economic policies that can encourage a pattern of developments which will generate sufficient jobs for the growing population, the list goes on. These challenges can tax all the ingenuity that we can muster. In the fields of political and social sciences, similar challenges present themselves, while international economic measures now in support of South

Africa will alleviate the financial stress of problem solving that we experienced in the past.

For those in search of adventure, excitement or opportunities to use their talents in a creative way, South Africa is clearly the place to be in future. The realisation that many of us have been privileged compared to the majority of our fellow citizens and that we have a head start in life that was given to us by the coincidence of being born into the more affluent part of our society, puts us under an obligation – *in fact we owe it to ourselves* – to use these advantages towards helping to create a better South Africa in which we can all look each other in the eyes and stand proud.

I wish you the best of luck in the choices you will make and would only ask that you be realistic about the evolutionary processes that our country is going through at present.

RULES OF THE GAME

The chaplain's advice to my son, John, on graduation day: "I am giving you the ball, son, and naming you the scrum half for your team in the game of life. I am your coach, so I'll give it to you straight.

There is only one game to play. It lasts all your life, with no time out and no substitutions. You play the whole game – all your life. You'll have a great backline and full back. You are calling the signals, but the other six fellows in the backline with you have great reputations. They are named Faith, Hope, Charity, Love, Peace and Commitment.

You'll work behind a truly powerful pack of forwards. End to end they consist of Honesty, Loyalty, Devotion to Duty, Self Respect, Sturdy Cleanliness, Good Behaviour, Courage and Enthusiasm.

The goal posts are the gates of heaven. God is the referee and sole official. He makes all the rules, and there is no appeal from them. There are ten rules. You know them as the Ten Commandments and you play them strictly in accordance with your own religion.

There is only one important ground rule. It is: *As ye would that men should do to you, do ye also to them likewise.*

Here is the ball. It is your immortal soul! Hold onto it. Now, son, get in there and let's see what you can do with it."

CHAPTER FIVE

THE WORLD AROUND US

CHAPTER FIVE

THE WORLD AROUND US

The next example is a condensed version of a talk given to 400 bankers at the University of South Africa. A patriotic theme was chosen because of the fear, uncertainty and doubt that prevailed shortly after the installation of South Africa's first democratic government. The title of the talk is *South Africa today*.

SOUTH AFRICA TODAY

Ladies and gentlemen, if I could make just one small stroke on the canvas of your lives today, then I would do it by reminding you that most of us, at some stage in our lives have left our most precious possessions, *our children*, in the care of a black nanny. I have never heard of a child who came to any harm while in their care. For generations now they have cooked our food, tended our homes and worked in our factories and offices. They have been loyal, obedient servants. They have displayed enormous goodwill towards us and it begs the questions, "Must I now be ashamed to take these people by the hand and walk to a new future together? Because we live on a daily diet of bad news, does this mean we must lose whatever sense of purpose that we might once have had?"

Has experience not taught us that when people of character have their backs to the wall, they defend themselves against all odds, and find solutions to their problems? South Africans are accustomed to finding solutions. We constantly use our talents to bring us back on track. Now for the first time in our history, we are free to openly debate any possibility. We can design South Africa in any way we like. The only barrier is our own unwillingness to let go of the past, to be bold enough to tackle the prospects of the future. We are not limited by resources, we are not short of opportunities, we cannot possibly turn back to what has failed, nor can we experiment with what has failed elsewhere. For too long we have tried to be the only white nation on a black continent. In the process we were maligned by our enemies and condemned by our friends.

For a brief moment in our history, we now have the opportunity to do almost anything. Let's grab that moment and make it work for us. We must take South Africa out of the economic morass it has been in for so long. The barrier of economic sanctions has been pushed aside, we have defied the world for long enough. We must now get on with Nation Building. We must display an attitude that will instill confidence and enthusiasm in everyone with whom we come into contact. We must make a spirited, passionate, positive attempt to remind people that we have a bright future before us. We must transform all our disappointments of the past into opportunities for the future. Our task is to help South Africans to right the great wrongs of the past.

The fulfilment of dreams lies partly in our capacity to identify opportunities and partly in the courage to grasp them before they slip away. South Africa is on the threshold of a great future. If we do not believe in miracles, we are not being realistic, to achieve our dreams we must accept the responsibility of every single day. *Our future begins today.* Aspirations have been awakened on this turbulent continent. To meet them, discipline and authority are necessary.

We must not see ourselves as being detached or isolated but rather as trustworthy members of society. We have been charged with the responsibility of facing a new challenge with many possibilities. We must make a conscious effort to grab every opportunity to create wealth and prosperity in our new country. We must be all-rounders in our rainbow nation.

Each one of us is a high profile person, which means that the future will to some extent be influenced by us. We are living in very exciting times. The old South Africa is dead and the new is only a few years old. Our new democracy neither doubts nor counts the cost of its new found freedom, but it asks of us to serve her with energy and purpose, and to be faithful to her, while keeping a cool head in the rough seas of Africa.

Let's pause for a moment and reflect on the past so that we can recognise some of the changes that have already been put into place. Looking back, our sports men and women became the *skunks of the world*. The French Rugby Team took a bold stand when they told us that either we play against Bougarell or we must be satisfied with bugger-all! We embarrassed New Zealand by buying their best rugby players to make up the clandestine rebel tour called the 'Cavaliers'.

As if that was not enough we refused Yvonne Goolagong and Arthur Ashe our tennis courts. Our own Basil D'Oliviera was good enough to play cricket for England but not for us. On the economic front, our businesses and factories were subjected to sanctions, embargoes and boycotts. No banker in the world would lend us money and we became accustomed to dealing in devious ways. Our business morality deteriorated and our factories were subsidised to enable them to produce goods that we could no longer import. Those subsidies filtered through to our wages, employment contracts and productivity until we were completely out of touch with reality.

This in turn affected other factories that did not qualify for government aid, they became less viable, stumbled and sometimes failed. Interest rates soared, unemployment was at a staggering high – taxation took off, all the signs of a sick economy were visible. Our military budget was enormous with thousands of kilometers of borders to patrol, electrify or plant land mines. Our raids in hot pursuit into Angola became every day occurrences and our sons were treated like traitors if they did not comply with their compulsory military training.

Tourism all but petered out. While a country to our north, Kenya, with very little to offer, was enjoying 2,9 million foreign tourists a year, we were attracting only 300 000.

We preferred to focus on the differences between our people rather than the common ground we shared. We developed a dinosaurian mentality, we refused to adapt or to change. Like ostriches, we would be quite content until trouble came and then we would stick our heads into the sand until the problem seemed to go away.

Our fellow South Africans pleaded desperately with us to include them as a part of our nation, to carry ID books instead of passes, to be accepted as normal human beings rather than second-rate temporary sojourners. We experienced Sharpeville, the Soweto riots, the Pretoria bomb and many, many other events, while our sons and daughters sacrificed themselves on the borders to keep us in cloud cuckoo land. We preferred to *die apart* than *live together*.

Eventually, only 13% of our population carried the burden for creating all the jobs, paying all the taxes and patrolling all our borders.

At last! The miracle of transformation started unfolding when negotiations commenced at the World Trade Centre.

The Westminster system was replaced by a new constitution, the misuse of power was effectively dealt with so that citizens could feel safe in their own country, and a more equitable dispensation was put into place assuring equal opportunities for all... *A New South Africa was born!*

Sports isolation ended and for the first time in living memory, all South Africans were united! We enjoyed one victory after another until it was climaxed by the Springboks winning the coveted World Cup. We became the champions of the world... what a moment to revere! Our cricketers hardly find time to change their underwear, they are so much in demand. What a pleasure seeing our athletes competing at all the international venues and bringing home the *Gold*.

Commerce and industry are re-positioning themselves for international trade and many of our national entrepreneurs are rapidly becoming multinationals. Foreign investors are once again looking at South Africa through different eyes, sometimes with a view to spring-boarding to Africa. The war has ended, inflation is down and we are adjusting to our new circumstances with people classified according to ability and not birth. We no longer legislate industry and commerce with restrictive laws that run counter to economic efficiency. Visitors to South Africa are struck by the energy with which policies are now discussed, the absent-mindedness, the inventiveness and the sincerity with which we debate in public how we should resolve our difficulties and face a future together.

Summarising, I would like to say that peaceful, orderly and evolutionary change in South Africa is not only desirable – *but fully attainable*. 'Quick fix' solutions to our problems are not always possible, some of our problems remain complex.

You do not have to be a modern-day Nostradamus to make your contribution to peaceful, evolutionary reform. Bartholomew Diaz did not know what lay ahead when he embarked on his journey around the southern tip of Africa. Neither did the 1820 Settlers nor the Voortrekkers have a clear vision of their future when they made their move. They made an intelligent assessment of the facts at their disposal, they accepted the realities of the situation, they considered different likely scenarios for the future, they placed their trust in the Almighty and acted in faith and with *enthusiasm*.

This is also the answer for South Africa today.

CHAPTER SIX

BIRTHDAYS

BIRTHDAYS

MY VERY SPECIAL FRIEND

Ladies and gentlemen, I was asked to propose a toast to the hero of the day. By accepting this invitation, I hope that I have not in any way implied that I think that I am the best qualified for the job. Nor do I think that I will be able to do justice to this occasion. On the contrary, my vocabulary is too limited to describe all the wonderful attributes of the man in whose honour we are gathered here.

No! I accepted this invitation for one reason only and that is because he is my very special friend. I know that he is also your very special friend – in fact, he is everybody's special friend. As far as I am concerned, *his friendship* is one of my most precious possessions. The high regard in which I hold him is shared by all who have contact with him, of that I am positive. His vision of the future and his capacity to understand some very complex situations have never ceased to amaze me, but, most of all, the confidence that he brings to his friends and colleagues is one of his finest attributes.

He is always a gentleman and sets a fine example – and is truly an all-weather friend that we can rely on. No words can do justice to him or for that matter explain the way we feel about him. Fortunately in the present company, it is not necessary because you all know him as well as I do. I shall therefore come straight to the point and ask you to be upstanding and to drink a toast to our wonderful friend. To your continued good health, happiness and prosperity, we say Happy Birthday to Martin.

THE METALLURGICAL AGE

Ladies and gentlemen, it is my pleasure to propose a toast to the birthday boy. At age 60, he is starting to enter the metallurgical age of a man, that is, the time when a man has more silver in his hair than in his pocket, more gold in his teeth than in the bank, and more lead in his feet than in his pencil. When Dennis was a younger man, he was a legend in his industry and there are still many wonderful stories told about his ability to sell motor cars.

On one occasion, he sold a used car to a priest and he told him that it was a most unusual vehicle. He said that, at a speed of 120 km an hour, the radio plays 'O bring me back to the old Transvaal', at 140 km an hour, it plays 'Nearer my God to thee', and at 180 km, it plays 'When the Roll is called up yonder I'll be there'.

A week later the priest brought the car back and asked Dennis if he could exchange it for a different one.
"Why?" Dennis asked.

"A priest cannot possibly drive around for too long in this car, it gives so much trouble that I am learning to use foul language already."

Dennis then moved to the Cape and started a little farming venture, where he made a million.

I asked him, "What would you do with all your money if you found out that tomorrow was Doomsday?"

As quick as a flash, he said, "Then I'll move to Pretoria because they are 20 years behind the times with everything and there I'll have a long time to enjoy my money."

Fortunately, money is not important to Dennis. He says that money can buy food – but not appetite; money can buy medicine – but not good health; money can buy a companion – but not a good friend; money can buy you peace – but not happiness. Ladies and gentlemen, no amount of money could make Dennis a better person than he already is.

I ask you all to charge your glasses, get on your feet and drink a toast to a most inspiring man. To Dennis, we wish you a long, happy and healthy life. Happy Birthday!

SEVENTY SOMETHING

Ladies and gentlemen, Jim no longer counts his years, but he knows he must be getting on, because this year it cost him more to buy the candles than the cake. He has been my *good friend* now for many years and I must tell you that *good friends* don't come any better. He's from that very special mould, the kind you don't find around much anymore. He's a walking encyclopedia, he can tell you all about the Great Depression of the 30's. He gets tears in his eyes when he hears Bing Crosby sing 'I'm dreaming of a white Christmas' and talks about 'Christmas puddings with tickeys in'.

He loved that old Austin 10, his first new car, and remembers buying cokes for a sixpence a bottle and two cigarettes for a penny. But look at him sitting there with his silver crown, as majestic as one can be, full of mischief and lots of fun – he's a great friend to have around.

Jim, our wish is that you will always stay as young as you are – remain healthy and have lots of fun. Ladies and gentlemen, a toast to Jim. Happy Birthday!

HEAVEN'S VERY SPECIAL CHILD

Ladies and gentlemen, to propose a toast to someone so special is always a great pleasure. Jonathan has succeeded, despite a handicap, when most normal children might have failed. He enjoys life and lives in an uncomplicated world. A world that only understands love, sincerity and loyalty. His life centres around his family, his friends and God.

He knows that Christ died for him on the cross and no complicated theology will deviate him from that belief. When God saw fit to set us here as friends and family of this fine young man He certainly had a purpose in mind, and that purpose was that Jonathan would touch our lives, in a very significant way. Each one of us has learnt that a healthy mind and a healthy body should not be taken for granted, it is a gift so precious that it comes straight to us from Heaven.

Jonathan does not pretend to understand the many things about tomorrow, but he knows who moulds tomorrow and he knows who holds his hand. He possesses the most natural beauty in the world – honest, moral truth. I came across a poem that captures it rather beautifully:

HEAVEN'S VERY SPECIAL CHILD

A meeting was held quite far from earth,
"It's time for another birth"
said the angels to the Lord above.
"This special child will need much love."

"His progress may seem very slow,
accomplishment he may not show,
and he'll require extra care
from the folks he meets down there."

"His thoughts may seem quite far away.
In many ways he won't adapt
and he'll be known as handicapped."

"So let's be careful where he's sent,
we want his life to be content.
Please Lord, find the parents who
will do a special job for you."

"They will not realize right away
the leading role they are asked to play.
But with this child sent from above,
comes stronger faith and richer love."

"And soon they'll know the privilege given
in caring for the gift from Heaven.
Their precious charge, so meek and mild,
it's Heaven's *very special child.*"
(AUTHOR UNKNOWN)

Ladies and gentlemen, we drink a toast to Jonathan.

ANY AGE

Ladies and gentlemen, life is very much like a train journey. Each year, when we celebrate your birthday, it is like stopping at a new station. We may have stopped at stations in the past called – *Going to school* or *Graduation* or more romantic stations called *Engagement party, Wedding or Honeymoon or even Parenthood!*

The train continues and we find stations called *Mother-in-law, Grandmother* and a lot of little sidings in between. Some of them are called *Happiness* and *Sorrow, Love, Hope* and *Charity.* If you enjoy a long life, the list of stations goes on and on!

Today we are celebrating *Station Number Eighty.* The train has just pulled in and we are all here on the platform to welcome Auntie Gwen to this important station in her life. Auntie Gwen, we have come to say how happy we are that you have arrived safely and in such good condition. We have also come to wish you a happy stay on *Station Number Eighty* and hope that you will continue to enjoy good health so that you can travel to many more wonderful destinations in the future.

Ladies and gentlemen, we drink to a well-travelled lady, Auntie Gwen.

85 YEARS YOUNG TODAY

In proposing a toast to this remarkable man, there are 101 beautiful things that could be said of him on the 85th anniversary of the day that

BIRTHDAYS

he was born. I am sure that he will forgive me if I only focus on one of his many attributes this evening, and that is *his love* for his children, grandchildren and great-grandchildren, and his fellow human beings. At a very tender age, he realised that the one thing in life that we all desperately need is *love*, not so much to receive it but to *give it*, because it is only through giving that we receive.

I always think of Gerrie Wessels when I hear that remarkable description of love in a letter from St. Paul to the Corinthians which reads: *If I have all the eloquence of men or of angels, but speak without love, I am simply a gong booming or a cymbal clashing.* St. Paul could almost be describing him as he continues because Gerrie Wessels has the gift of prophecy, understanding, faith in all its fullness and *above all, love.*

He is always patient and kind, he is not boastful or conceited, he is never rude or selfish, resentful or offensive and he always delights in the truth.

I was not surprised when his grandson, Jonathan, while visiting with us the other day was talking about his relationship with the church and said, "If I am a child of God today, then it is because I have a grandfather like Gerrie Wessels."

Dear friends and family, notwithstanding the fact that this man is 85 years old today, he starts every day geared to the future. He is a man who has warmed both his hands at the flame of eternity, he has lived a full and useful life. He continues to dream dreams and has a wonderful sense of humour, and now I want to shower him with the following words.

Gerrie, expect the best, life is not over yet, and remember that God always keeps the best wine for last. That unknown author of these beautiful words must have had you in mind when he wrote,

"I shall pass this way but once. Any good, therefore, that I can do, or any kindness that I can show to any human being, let me do it now, let me not defer or neglect it for I shall not pass this way again."

Ladies and gentlemen, please rise and drink a toast to this *grand young man*. To Gerrie Wessels.

CHAPTER SEVEN

GOLDEN OLDY TRIVIA

GOLDEN OLDY TRIVIA

EVOLUTION AS A MONKEY SEES IT

Three monkeys sat in a coconut tree,
Discussing things as they're said to be.
Said one to the others, "Now listen, you two,
There's a certain rumour, that can't be true,
That man descended from our noble race;
The very idea is an utter disgrace.
No monkey ever deserted his wife,
Starved her babies, or ruined her life.
And you've never heard of another monk
Who left her babies with others to bunk,
Or passed them on from one to another
'Til they scarcely knew which was their mother.

And, another thing, you'll never see
A monk build a fence round a coconut tree,
Forbidding all monks a taste
Of coconut milk with whisky laced.
If I'd built a fence around that tree,
Starvation would force you to steal from me.
And another thing a monk won't do
Is to go out at night and go on the stew,
Or use a gun, or club or knife
To take some other monkey's life.
Yes, man descended – the onery cuss -
But brother, he didn't descend from us."

METHUSELAH

Methuselah ate what he found on his plate
and never as people do now,
did he check the amount of the calorie counts
he ate it because it was chow.
He wasn't disturbed when at dinner he sat
devouring a roast or a pie,
to think it was lacking in granular fat
or a couple of vitamins shy.
He therefore chewed every species of food
unmindful of trouble or fear
lest his health might be hurt
by some fancy dessert
and he lived over ninety full years.'
(AUTHOR UNKNOWN)

Terminal patients were asked to write an essay entitled "If I had my life over again, how would I live it?"

AN 85-YEAR-OLD, DYING FROM CANCER, WROTE THIS:

If I had my life to live over again I'd not be afraid of more mistakes. Next time, in fact, I'd relax more, I'd be sillier than I was on this trip. As a matter of fact, I know of very few things that I would take so seriously.
I'd take more chances – more trips. Climb more mountains.
I'd swim more rivers – I'd sit and watch more sunsets – go to more places I'd never seen before.
Eat more ice cream instead of beans.
I'd have more actual troubles and fewer imaginary ones.
Ninety per cent of the things we worry about never happen – and yet we worry and we worry.
Worry when it's there.
Do something about it when it's there.

I lived so sensibly – hour after hour, day after day – I had my moments.
And if I had my life over again I'd have more moments.

I'd try to have nothing else but wonderful moments.
Instead of living so many years ahead of my time.
I never went anywhere without a thermometer – a hot water bottle, a gargle, a raincoat and a parachute.

If I had to do it all over again I would travel lighter.
If I had my life over again I'd play with more children – pick more daisies and love more; if I had my life over again, but you see. I don't – we are given only one. To be is to do and to do is to do it now.

AGE IS A QUALITY OF MIND

Age is a quality of mind
If you have left your dreams behind
If hope is cold
If you no longer plan ahead
If your ambitions are all dead
Then you are old

But if you make of life the best,
And in your life you still have zest,
If love you hold –
no matter how the years go by,
no matter how the birthdays fly,
you are not old
(AUTHOR UNKNOWN)

YOUTH AND AGE

Some people die *old* at 20 and get buried at 80, others die *young* at 80 but only after they have lived life to the full. This strange phenomena is explained in one word *attitude*. Being young is not having a youthful complexion, a sun-tanned body or supple knees, but the quality of your ideas, your thoughts and the vitality of your passion. Nobody grows old simply because of accumulating years, but by giving up on your dreams, hopes, loves , wants and desires.

GOLDEN OLDY TRIVIA

In all of our hearts you will find an attraction for *what is next* in the game of life, the appetite for being that boundless infant saying, "never say die!", who continues to radiate hope, courage and beauty even long after the body's skin has wrinkled and the joints move painfully slowly. To manifest this fountain of youth in your heart requires only one word *'attitude'*. Yes, your frame of mind more than anything else will determine your youthfulness at any age in life. Youth means your ability to control your courage, your fears and your freshness of thought. Nobody has ever left this world alive, so why wrinkle your soul by giving up on enthusiasm. When you wake up in the morning, say, *"It's time to get up"* and not "My time is up".

Turn your face to the future today and let those love you who never loved you before and those who always loved you, love you even more.

THE PRESERVATION OF MAN

The horse and the mule live 30 years,
And nothing know of wines and beers.
The goat and sheep at twenty die with never a taste of scotch or rye.
The cow drinks water by the ton and at 18 is mostly done.
The dog at 16 cashes in without the aid of rum or gin.
The cat in milk and water soaks and then in 12 short years it croaks.
The modest, sober, bone dry hen lays eggs for nogs, then dies at ten.
All animals are strictly dry, they sinless live and swiftly die.
But sinful, ginful, rum-soaked men
Survive for three score years and ten
And some of us, the mighty few,
stay pickled till we're 92.
(AUTHOR UNKNOWN)

YES, I'M TIRED

For several years, I've been blaming it on middle age, poor blood circulation, lack of vitamins, air pollution, saccharine, obesity, dieting, under arm odour, yellow wax build-up, the ozone and another dozen maladies that make you wonder if life is really worth living.

BUT! I found out it ain't that at all.
I'm tired because I am overworked.
The population of this country is 51 million

21 million are retired.
That leaves 30 million to do the work.

There are 19 million at school.
That leaves 11 million to do the work.
Three million are unemployed and four million are employed by the Government.
That leaves five million to do the work.
One million are in the Armed Forces, which leaves four million to do the work.
Three million are employed by Country and Borough Councils, leaving one million to do the work.
There are 620 000 people in the hospitals, and 379 998 in prison.
Which leaves two people to do the work

You and ME???
You're sitting on your backside reading this!

... NO WONDER I'M BLOODY TIRED!!!

WHEN ARE YOU OLD?

A senior citizen is one who was here before television, frozen foods, credit cards, ball point pens and the Pill.

For us 'time-sharing' meant togetherness, and a 'chip' was a piece of wood. 'Hardware' meant hard wear and 'software' was not even a word. Teenagers never wore slacks or jeans. We were there before pantyhose, drip dry clothes, dishwashers, clothes driers and electric blankets.

We got married first, then lived together. We thought cleavage was something butchers did. We were here before Batman, disposable nappies, jeeps, pizzas, instant coffee and KFC.

In our days, cigarette smoking was fashionable, grass was for mowing, pot was something one cooked in, a gay person was the life and soul of the party, and aids were right-hand people...

We are today's senior citizens – a hardy bunch when you think of how the world has changed and the adjustments we have had to make!

HOW DO YOU KNOW WHEN YOU ARE GROWING OLD?

Everything hurts – what doesn't hurt, doesn't work.
The gleam in your eye is the sun glinting on your bifocals.
You feel like the morning after, but haven't been anywhere.
Your little Black Book only contains names ending with M.D.
You get winded playing cards.
Your children begin to look middle-aged.
You join a health club but don't go.
A dripping tap causes an uncontrollable urge.
You know all the answers but nobody asks the questions.
You look forward to a dull evening.
You need glasses to find your glasses.
You turn out the light for economy, instead of romance.
You sit in a rocking chair but can't make it go.
Your knees buckle but your belt won't.
Your back goes out more than you do.
You put your bra on back to front and it fits better.
Your house is too big and your medicine chest
not big enough.
You sink your teeth into a steak and they stay there.
Your birthday cake collapses under the weight
of the candles.

I can cope with my arthritis
my false teeth are not a bind
I can cope with my bi-focals
But gosh, I miss my mind.
(ANONYMOUS)

REMEMBER

Old folks are worth a fortune, with silver on their heads, gold in their teeth, stones in their kidneys, lead in the feet, and gas in their stomachs.

I have become a little older since I saw you last and a few changes have come in my life since then. Frankly, I have become a frivolous old girl. I am seeing two men each day; as soon as I wake up, Will Power helps me get out of bed. When he leaves, Arthur Itis shows up and stays the rest of the day. He doesn't stay in one place very long, so he takes me from joint to joint. The preacher came to call the other day. He said that at my age I should be thinking about the hereafter. I told him I do so all the time. No matter where I am, in the parlour, upstairs, in the kitchen or down in the basement, I ask myself, "What am I here after?"

HOW DO YOU KNOW?

How does a man know when he is growing old?
When he can't take yes for an answer

AT DAY'S END

Is anyone happier because you passed this way? Does anyone remember that you spoke to him today?
The day is almost over, and its toiling time is through!
Is there anyone to utter now a kindly word to you?
Can you say tonight, in parting with the day that's slipping fast, that you helped a single person of the many that you passed?

Is a single heart rejoicing over what you did or said?
Does a man whose hopes were fading, now with courage look ahead?
Did you waste the day or lose it? Was it well or sorely spent?
Did you leave a trail of kindness, or a scar of discontent?
As you close your eyes in slumber, do you think that God will say:
"You have earned one more tomorrow by the work you did today?"
J. HALL

A TOUCH OF WICKEDNESS

My rookie days are over
My pilot light is out
What used to be my sex appeal
Is now my water spout.

Time was when of its own accord
From my trousers it would spring
But now I have a full-time job
To find the blasted thing.

It used to be embarrassing
The way it would behave
For every single morning
It would stand and watch me shave.

As my old age approaches
It sure gives me the blues
To see it hang its little head
And watch me tie my shoes.

Senior citizens are the nation's leading carriers of aids!
Hearing aids, band aids, roll aids, walking aids,
Medical aids and, most of all,
Monetary aid to their children.

The golden years have come at last!
I cannot see, I cannot pee, I cannot chew
I cannot screw.
My memory shrinks. My hearing stinks
No sense of smell
I look like hell!
My body's drooping, got trouble pooping
So, the golden years have come at last?
Well, the golden years can kiss my arse!

IT'S ALL IN YOUR MIND

From 20 to 30 if things
go right ...
It's once in the morning
and once at nite! ...

From 30 to 40 you're
still going strong ...
Half as often but
twice as long!

From 40 to 50 your
inclinations
are Saturday nights
and summer vacations!
From 50 to 60 it's just
bi-weekly ...

From 60 to 70
you just try meekly!

After that if you're
still inclined
just take a cold shower,
it's all in your mind!

My wife never lies about her age. She just tells people she's as old as I am, then she lies about my age.

I'm growing old all by myself. My wife hasn't had a birthday in ten years.

At 70 there are ten women for every man – what a time to get odds like that.

The best time for men to have babies is when they are 70. That's when they have to get up ten times a night anyway.

This is the age when a man's mind turns from passion to pension.

His wife powders and he puffs.

He's gone from why not, to why bother.

CHAPTER SEVEN

His uncle died the other day at 104. He was shot by a jealous husband. His aunt died at 102 – thank God, they saved the baby.

Peter elbowed me and asked, "Are you going to speak now?"
His wife replied, "No – let our friends enjoy themselves for a while longer."

I'm not very fond of speaking, but Wendy and I have been married for 40 years – and this may be my only opportunity to say a few words.

I AM FINE

There is nothing the matter with me
I'm as healthy as can be
I have arthritis in both knees
And when I talk, I talk with a wheeze
My pulse is weak and my blood is thin
But I'm awfully well for the shape I'm in.

GOLDEN OLDY TRIVIA

Arch supports I have for my feet
Or I wouldn't be able to walk in the street
Sleep is denied me night after night
But every morning I find I'm alright.
My memory is fading, my head's in a spin
But I'm awfully well for the shape I'm in.
The moral of this tale I unfold
That for me and you who are growing old,
It's better to say I'm fine with a grin
Than to let folks know the shape we are in.

How do I know that my youth is all spent?
Well, my get up and go has got up and went.
But I really don't mind when I think with a grin
Of all the grand places my get up has been.

Old age is golden I've heard said
But sometimes I wonder as I get into bed.
With my ears in a drawer, my teeth in a cup
My eyes on the table until I get up.
Ere sleep overcomes me I say to myself
Is there anything else I could put on the shelf?

When I was young, my slippers were red,
I could kick my heels right over my head.
When I grew older my slippers were blue
But still I could dance the whole night through.
Now, when I'm old, my slippers are black
I walk to the store and puff my way back.

I get up each morning and dust off my wits,
Pick up the papers and read the obits.
But if my name is missing, I know I'm not dead,
So I eat a good breakfast and go back to bed.
(AUTHOR UNKNOWN)

CHAPTER EIGHT

EULOGIES

"PEOPLE ARE DYING TO RIDE IN THESE CARS"

EULOGIES

EULOGY TO ROGER BOUSTRED

On behalf of the family and friends, I would, first of all, like to convey our heartfelt sorrow to Margaret and the children. Your loss is our loss, your grief is our grief and Margaret, we express our deepest sympathy to you and your daughters on this sad day.

Roger was a friend and colleague of mine, we had worked together for many years. In fact, when I came into the real estate business, he was my mentor. He was a practical man and a true professional, he loved his work and was very successful at it. He made many friends and was an advisor to most of the larger financial institutions on property matters.

His passing has brought to an end the dreadful suffering that he had to endure this past year. We are all happy that at last he has been relieved of this discomfort and he is now in a place where there is no more suffering and no more pain. While the priest was quoting from the scriptures this morning that well-known passage... "In my Father's home, there are many mansions, I go to prepare a place for you", I couldn't help feeling that God in his wisdom must have invested heavily in Real Estate up there and he now needs a good man to take care of those mansions and so he took the best. I am sure that Roger will be delighted to serve him.

Death is not a dark and sinister state, on the contrary, we have all been taught that eternal life can only begin after death. His departure from earth will leave a void that will not be easy to fill, but fortunately the memory of his smiling, friendly face will console us until we meet again.

On behalf of the family, may I express a sincere word of thanks to Father O'Reilly for his comforting words and his lovely service. To the doctors and nurses at the hospital who treated Roger with such tender loving care during his last few days, to the funeral undertakers who went about their work so professionally, to the many people whose messages, flowers and offers of assistance during this time gave Margaret and the girls great support and it was much appreciated. Last but not least, to each one of you for taking time off to be here this morning to support the family, thank you very much.

Will you please switch on your car headlights as the cortege moves towards the cemetery. Traffic officers will be on duty to assist and it will make their job so much easier if they can identify you.

EULOGY TO PAT MCGRATH

I would like to say how very sad we are today, at having to say goodbye to our friend, Pat McGrath. We know that it is even more difficult for Estelle, Karen and Andrew to say goodbye to their father, loved one and head of the household. We share in their grief and sorrow and pray that God will give them the strength to carry on with their lives.

Pat was a family man and loyal friend to all of us, I will miss the companionship that I enjoyed so much during the past 30 years. If it were possible for me to speak to Pat this morning and ask him what he would like me to say, he would probably say... "Tell them that I am happy because I have arrived home, tell them that there is a wonderful reason for death because without death, eternal life cannot begin, but equally important... death creates an urgency on earth for us to say to one another 'I love you'. If it were not for death, we would put it off for another day – another week maybe even next year, until it was too late." We can't tell Pat we love him anymore, because for him it is too late, so why not learn from Pat's death this morning... don't put it off any longer.

If you are sitting next to your wife, your girlfriend or just a friend this morning – turn to one another now and say 'I love you'. Do it! And every time from now on when you use or hear those three little words, think of Pat.

CHAPTER EIGHT

I came across a poem by Charles Hanson Towne which I have adapted slightly. It sums it up!

Around the corner I have a friend,
In this great city that has no end;
Yet days go by, and weeks rush on,
And before I know it a year has gone,
And I never see my old friend's face,
For life is a swift and terrible race.
He knows I like him just as well
As in the days when I rang his bell
And he rang mine. We were younger then,
And now we are busy, tired men;
Tired with playing a foolish game,
Tired with trying to make a name.
"Tomorrow" I say, "I will call on Pat
Then he and I can have a chat."
But tomorrow comes – and tomorrow goes,
And the distance between us grows and grows.

Around the corner – yet miles away ...
"Here's a telegram, sir..."
"Pat died today."

And that's what we get, and deserve in the end:
Around the corner, a vanished friend.

CHAPTER NINE

INSPIRATIONAL STUFF

CHAPTER NINE

INSPIRATIONAL STUFF

Very often we don't have the time to relax with a good inspirational book to remind us of those important little things in life that give us hope and reason to carry on. This section is a quick-start, easy read, which reminds us that our journey is about laughing together, loving each other, seeking adventure, believing in our dreams and making a difference. Life's little reminders are there to convince us that we are bigger than anything that can happen to us.

A TOAST

I might wish you wealth;
or, might wish you health;
or, that good fortune would caress you.
But wealth might bring sorrow,
and health could fail – tomorrow;
so, I'll simply say, God bless you!

WHEN GOD GAVE OUT BRAINS

When God gave out brains, I thought he said trains
    And I missed mine.
When God gave out looks, I thought he said books
    And I didn't want any.
When God gave out ears, I thought he said beers
    So I ordered two large ones.
When God gave out chins, I thought he said gins
    So I ordered a double
When God gave out legs, I thought he said kegs
    And I asked for two fat ones.
When God gave out heads, I thought he said beds
    So I asked for a soft one.

No wonder I'm such a mess!

TIME TO PRAY

I got up early one morning
And rushed right into the day
I had so much to accomplish
That I didn't have time to pray
Problems came tumbling about me
And heavier came each task
"Why doesn't God help me?" I wondered
He answered, "You didn't ask"

I wanted to see joy and beauty
But the day toiled on, grey and bleak
I wondered why God didn't show me
He said, "But you didn't seek"

I tried to come into God's presence
I used all my keys at the lock
God kindly and lovingly chided
"My child, you didn't knock"

I woke up early this morning
And paused before entering the day
I had so much to accomplish
That I had to make time to pray
A. DODDS

FOOTPRINTS IN THE SAND

"One night a man had a dream. He dreamt he was walking along the beach with the Lord. Across the sky flashed scenes from his life. For each scene he noticed two sets of footprints in the sand. One set belonged to him, the other to the Lord."

When the last scene of his life flashed before him, he looked back at the footprints in the sand. He noticed that many times along the path of life there was only one set of footprints. He also noticed it happened at the very lowest and saddest times in his life.

This really bothered him and he questioned the Lord about it. "Lord, You said that once I decided to follow you, you would walk with me all the way. But, I have noticed that during the most troublesome times in my life, there is only one set of footprints. I do not understand why in the times I needed You most, You would leave me.

The Lord replied,

"My precious, precious child, I
Love you and I would never
Leave you. During your times
Of trial and suffering, when
You saw only one set of footprints,
It was when I carried you!

INSPIRATIONAL STUFF

STATEMENT OF FAITH

I believe there was a wonderful man who lived a wonderful life. He died and now he lives again. And I believe that because he did it, I can do it – that's the way I believe it, and I am not going to let anybody mess it up with so much theology that I don't understand it.

THE SERMON ON THE MOUNT

Blessed are the poor in spirit: for theirs is the kingdom of heaven. Blessed are they that mourn: for they shall be comforted. Blessed are the meek: for they shall inherit the earth. Blessed are they that hunger and thirst after righteousness: for they shall be filled. Blessed are the merciful: for they shall obtain mercy. Blessed are the pure in heart: for they shall see God. Blessed are the peacemakers: for they shall be called sons of God.

Blessed are they that have been persecuted for righteousness' sake: for theirs is the kingdom of heaven. Blessed are ye when men shall reproach you, and persecute you, and say all manner of evil against you falsely, for my sake. Rejoice, and be exceeding glad: for great is your reward in heaven.

THE GOLDEN THREAD

Christianity: Matthew Chapter 7 verse 12
"All things whatsoever ye would that men should do to you, do ye even to them; for this is the law and the prophets."

Judaism: Talmud, Shabbatt 31a
"What is hateful to you, do not to your fellowman. That is the entire law; all the rest is commentary."

Islam: Sunnah
"No one of you is a believer until he desires for his brother that which he desires for himself."

Brahmanism: Mahabharata 5, 1517
"This is the sum of duty; do naught unto others which could cause you pain if done to you."

Buddhism: Udana-Varga 5, 18
"Hurt not others in ways that you yourself would find hurtful."

Confucianism: Analects 15, 23
"Is there one maxim which ought to be acted upon throughout one's whole life? Surely it is the maxim of loving kindness; do not unto others what you would not have them do unto you."

Taoism: T'ai Shang Kan Ying P'ien
"Regard your neighbour's gain as your own, and your neighbour's loss as your own loss."

Zoroastrianism: Dadistan-I-dinik 94, 5
"That nature alone is good which refrains from doing unto others whatsoever is not good for itself."

HEAVEN'S GROCERY STORE

I was walking down life's highway a long time ago
When one day I saw a sign that read "Heaven's Grocery Store";
As I got a little closer, the door came open wide,
And when I came to myself, I was standing inside.

I saw a host of angels – they were standing everywhere;
One handed me a basket, and said, "My child, shop with care."
Everything a Christian needed was in the Grocery Store
And all you couldn't carry, you could come back next day for;

First I got some *Patience* – Love was in the next row;
Further down was *Understanding* – you need that everywhere you go.
I got a box or two of *Wisdom*, a bag or two of *Faith*;
I couldn't miss the *Holy Spirit* – He was everywhere.

And then I stopped to get some *Strength* and *Courage*
To help me run the race;
By then my basket was getting full, but I remembered I needed some *Grace*
I didn't forget *Salvation*, for Salvation – that was free,

So I tried to get enough of that to save for both you and me.
Then I headed for the till to pay my grocery bill,
For I thought I had everything to do my Master's will.
But then I saw a *Prayer* and just had to put that in,

For I knew that when I stepped outside I'd run right into sin.
Peace and *Joy* were plentiful – they were on the last shelf;
Songs and *Praise* were hanging near, so I helped myself.
Then I said to the Angel "Now how much do I owe?"

He smiled and said "Just take them everywhere you go."
Again I asked him "Really, how much do I owe?"
He smiled the same and said: "My child, don't you know?
Jesus paid your bill a long time ago."

WHAT IS CHARITY?

It's Silence when your words will hurt
It's Patience when your neighbour is curt
It's Deafness when a scandal flows
It's Thoughtfulness for others' woes
It's Promptness when stern duty calls
It's Courage when misfortune falls
(SOURCE UNKNOWN)

AN IRISH BLESSING

May the road
rise to meet you
May the wind be
always at your back
May the sun shine
warm upon your face
May the rains fall
soft upon your fields
and, until
we meet again
May God hold you
in the palm of His hand

DEAR FRIEND

Dear friend,

How are you? I just had to send a note to tell you how much I love you and care about you.

I saw you yesterday as you were walking with your friends. I waited all day hoping you would want to walk with me also. As evening drew near I gave you a sunset to close your day and a cool breeze to rest you, and I waited. You never came. Yes, it did hurt me, but I still love you because I am your friend.

I saw you fall asleep last night and longed to touch you, so I spilled moonlight upon your pillow and face. Again I waited, wanting to rush down so we could talk. I have so many gifts for you. You awakened late and rushed off to work. My tears were in the rain. Today you look so sad, so all alone. It makes my heart ache because I understand. My friends let me down and hurt me so many times too, but I love you.

INSPIRATIONAL STUFF

Oh, if you would only listen to me. *I love you*. I try to tell you in the blue sky and in the quiet green grass. I whisper it in the leaves on the trees and breathe it in the colours of the flowers. I shout it to you in the mountain streams and give the birds love songs to sing.

I clothe you with warm sunshine and perfume the air with nature's scents. My love for you is deeper than the oceans and bigger than the biggest want or need in your heart. Oh! If only you knew how much I want to help you. I want you to meet my Father he wants to help you too. My Father is that way, you know.

Just call me, ask me, talk to me. Oh please, please don't forget me. I have so much to share with you. Okay, I won't hassle you any further. You are free to choose me. It is your decision. I have chosen you, and because of this I will wait, because *I love you*.

Your friend,
Jesus

LIMITS OF PARENTHOOD

I give you life, but I cannot live it for you.
I can teach you things, but I cannot make you learn.
I can give you directions, but I cannot be there to lead you.
I can allow you freedom, but I cannot account for it.
I can take you to church, but I cannot make you believe.
I can teach you right and wrong, but I cannot decide for you.
I can buy a beautiful garment, but I cannot make you beautiful inside.
I can offer you advice, but I cannot accept it for you.
I can give you love, but I cannot force it upon you.
I can teach you to share, but I cannot make you unselfish.
I can teach you respect, but I cannot force you to show honour.
I can advise you about friends, but I cannot choose them for you.
I can advise you about sex, but I cannot keep you pure.
I can tell you the facts of life, but I cannot build your reputation.
I can tell you about drink, but I can't say no for you.
I can warn you about drugs, but I can't prevent you from using them.
I can tell you about lofty goals, but I can't achieve them for you.
I can teach you about kindness, but I can't force you to be gracious.
I can warn you about sins, but I cannot make you moral.
I can love you as a child, but I cannot place you in God's family.
I can pray for you, but I cannot make you walk with God.
I can teach you about Jesus, but I cannot make Jesus your Lord.
I can tell you how to live, but I cannot give you eternal Life.

CHILDREN LIVE WHAT THEY LEARN

If a child lives with criticism
He learns to condemn
If a child lives with ridicule
He learns to be shy
If a child lives with shame
He learns to be guilty
If a child lives with fairness
He learns justice
If a child lives with encouragement
He learns confidence
If a child lives with security
He learns to have faith
If a child lives with approval
He learns to appreciate
If a child lives with acceptance and friendship
He learns to find love in the world.

MOTHERS' DAY

When all is said, it is the mother, and the mother only, who is a better citizen than the soldier who fights for his country. The successful mother, the mother who does her part in rearing and training aright the boys and girls who are to be men and women of the next generation, is of the greater use to the community, and occupies, if she would only realize it, a more honourable as well as a more important position than any man in it. The mother is the one supreme asset of the national life. She is more important, by far, than the successful statesman, or businessman, or artist, or scientist.
T. ROOSEVELT

ISN'T LIFE GLORIOUS!

Isn't life glorious! Isn't it grand!
Here, take it – hold it tight in your hand,
Squeeze every drop of it into your soul.
Drink of the joy of it, sun-sweet and whole.
Laugh with the love of it, burst into song!
Scatter its richness as you stride along!
Isn't life splendid and isn't it great,
You can always start living,
It's never too late.
(AUTHOR UNKNOWN)

CHAPTER TEN

SUCCESS

CHAPTER TEN

SUCCESS

WHAT SUCCESS IS ALL ABOUT

Ladies and gentlemen, the only place in the world where you will find success before hard work is... in the dictionary. Generally speaking, the word *success* is associated with hard work. It is said that man was designed for accomplishment, engineered for success and is endowed with the seeds of greatness. But no amount of human qualities can substitute knowledge or facts and skills. These elements are essential to success. Picture it this way, if you have the *knowledge and skills* then you are wearing one boxing glove, if you have the human qualities you are wearing a second boxing glove and with both gloves on, when you get into the ring of life you can win.

We all agree that there is little one can learn from doing nothing, so we create challenges and we find people who are prepared to accept them. Success however, means different things to different people. For example, for the boxer it may mean a world title, an athlete, a gold medal at the Olympic Games; for a doctor, putting new life into an almost dead body and a gardener, driving a motorized lawn mower, while to a tramp... perhaps just another bottle of wine.

Success does not have a meaning that can be superimposed on everyone. You may start off with a few small successes and graduate into major successes. As a businessman, I may be a success because I have accumulated a million but as a gardener, I could be a horrible failure. So it is quite possible to be a success and a failure at the same time. Do you know who the luckiest people in the world are? The ones who love what they are doing and the people that they are working with. A successful person is one who makes others feel good just because they are there.

I came across the following outline which really makes a lot of sense to me. It is called *IF* (with apologies to Rudyard Kipling)

If you choose to work, you will succeed. If you don't, you will fail! If you neglect your work, you will dislike it. If you enjoy it, you will do it well. If you join little cliques, you will be self-satisfied. If you make friends widely, you will be interesting. If you gossip you will be slandered. If you mind your own business, you will be defended. If you act like a human being, you will be respected. If you spurn wisdom, people will spurn you. If you seek wisdom, they will seek you. If you adopt the pose of boredom, you will be a bore. If you show vitality, you will be alive. If you spend your free time playing bridge, you will become a very good bridge player. If you spend it reading, discussing and thinking of things that matter, you will be an educated person.

Some of us become obsessed with a desire to succeed. Obsession at its extreme is a form of madness. This implies that sometimes we are prepared to go to the extreme, take a rather unnatural view. The person who is willing to sacrifice his wife – his children – his friends – his health and even his life to succeed. That kind of success has no place in my approach but I must concede that I have known such people, they pay very dearly for their success. And find themselves using their cheque books as the only way to solve their problems. Money becomes everything in their lives and as one successful cheque-book entrepreneur put it, "money is not everything in life, but it's far ahead of whatever comes second".

I prefer the expression of success that is captured in the poem by an unknown author:

SUCCESS

Success is speaking words of praise,
In cheering other people's ways,
In doing just the best you can,
With every task and every plan,
It's silence when your speech would hurt,
Politeness when your neighbour's curt,
It's loyalty when duty calls,
It's courage when disaster falls,
It's patience when the hours are long,
It's found in laughter and in song,
It's in the silent time of prayer,
In happiness and in despair,
In all of life and nothing less,
We find the thing we call *success*.
(AUTHOR UNKNOWN)

We are on the road to success when we realise a few basic principles. You must:

1. Know what you want to be successful at
2. Want it with all your heart
3. You may have to sacrifice something to achieve it
4. You must enjoy getting there
5. Do what you are doing with confidence, enthusiasm and pride
6. Be prepared to listen, to be humble and courteous.

Success is simply attaining what you set out to do. You may have a successful shopping spree – you may have a successful day, week, month, year or life. We must fight the tendency to look at others to see how far they have come. The only thing that counts is how we use our potential, how we run our race and whether or not we are using our best ability. Success is not a pie, with a number of slices to go around. The success of others is nothing to do with our success. Nor is it measured by what others say or what they accomplish. We all have a tendency to compare ourselves with others, but the happy people in life know that it's not against

SUCCESS

others that we compete. After all, a thoroughbred horse, once in a race, never looks around, he just concentrates on running that race. Each one of us is on our own track of success.

The race of life lasts for three score years and ten and if you are very healthy, a little longer. To win all the way requires staying power. Success is not about being 'lucky'. A successful engineer can walk onto a site and without much effort say "These people are losing money". Through years of practical work, he can sense there's something wrong. He knows his job so well that it becomes like instinct, an extra faculty. Similarly, a successful accountant who knows his work, can look at a control system and without much effort will say, "This system won't work".

Human qualities are important but equally important is knowledge. The catalyst that makes these two components gel is *enthusiasm.*

You can do anything if you have
Enthusiasm.. Enthusiasm is the
Yeast that makes your hopes
Rise to the stars

Enthusiasm is the sparkle in your
Eye, it is the swing in your gait,
The grip of your hand, the
Irresistible surge of your will and
Your energy to execute your ideas

Enthusiasts are fighters. They have
Fortitude – they have staying qualities
Enthusiasm is at the bottom of
All progress. With it there is
Accomplishment, without it there
Are only alibis
(AUTHOR UNKNOWN)

It is your attitude at the beginning of a task more than anything else that will determine your success or failure. It is your attitude towards life, which will determine life's attitude towards you. Life plays no favourites.

You and you alone control your attitude. Before you can develop a positive attitude, you must remember that action triggers feelings and feelings trigger actions; so why not act positively, think positively, walk, talk and conduct yourself in the attitude that you wish to assume and soon you will become that person.

Treat everyone as if they are very important and see how quickly your life changes. Accept the fact that there are more reasons why you should succeed than why you should fail. When you are faced with a problem, adopt the attitude that you can and will solve it. Control your thoughts and you will control your life. Radiate confidence and look like a person who knows where he/she is going. When you wake up in the morning, say, "Good Morning, Lord" and not "Good Lord, it's morning". It's not what happens to you in life that is important, it's how you take it. You are now on the *brink of success* and it's good to remember that it's wonderful to have money and the things that money can buy. But once in a while we must remember that *you must not lose the things that money cannot buy. Don't pay* the price of success, enjoy the price of success.

Beware of the disease called success. Don't let your groove become your grave! Rather learn to become a team player and to do more for the people you care about. Take up the challenge, think big! Most people think small because they are afraid of success. Being sure of oneself immediately gives one a great advantage.

Finally, let me give you a recipe that will enable you to succeed with "E's".

SUCCEED WITH "E'S"

Education is the safest plan
Expand on it whenever you can
Enrich your brain with all those tools
Excluded from the minds of fools

Enthuse your fellow human beings
Excite them with your goals and dreams
Establish who, what, why, when and where
Essential if you really care

Encourage those, who when you meet
Erupt with tales of their defeat
Evaluate their reasons why
Embrace those lessons until you die

Enjoy the fruits of life that come
Exclusive to the few that won
Endurance through adversity
Emerges from all history

Escape the ranks of "labour in vain"
Embark on a "plan of action" again
Everyone stands aside for a man
Especially for one who knows that he can

Endear yourself to the task at hand
Ethically bound by the laws of the land
Expect the best but give yours too
Exalting the status of what you do

Everyone following these simple rules
Employing their talents and these little jewels
Explode with vigour in varying degrees
Eager to win and succeed with E's.
(AUTHOR UNKNOWN)

CHAPTER ELEVEN

SUCCESS TRIVIA

SUCCESS TRIVIA

THE GUY IN THE GLASS

When you get what you want in your struggle for self
And the world makes you king for a day,
Then go to the mirror and look at yourself
And see what that guy has to say.

For it isn't your mother, your father or wife
Whose judgement on you must pass.
The fellow whose verdict counts most in your life
Is the guy staring back from the glass.

He's the fellow to please, never mind all the rest
For he's with you clean to the end;
And you've passed your most dangerous and
Difficult test if the guy in the glass is your friend.

You may be like Jack Horner and chisel a plum
And think you are a wonderful guy,
But the guy in the glass says you are a bum
If you can't look him straight in the eye.

You may fool the whole world, down the pathway of years
And get pats on the back as you pass;
But the final reward will be heartaches and tears
If you've cheated the guy in the glass.
ANONYMOUS

THE FOUR SENSES OF SUCCESS

1. Common sense
2. Sense of humour
3. Sense of balance
4. Sense of value

Put together means: we do the ordinary things better!

A SIMPLE FORMULA FOR SUCCESS

S   Start thinking, is this just a job or is it your career?

U   You need to get further education yourself.

C   Compensation. Understand exactly how you are paid.

C   Communication and caring. Develop these skills.

E   Effort. You can't build a good reputation on what you are going to do. You have to do it!

S   Stress. Learn how to handle it.

S   Secret of success. Do your personal best and never settle for less.

Success is an objective achieved!

DON'T QUIT

When things go wrong as they sometimes will,
When the road you are trudging seems all uphill,
When funds are low and the debts are high,
And you want to smile but you had to sigh,
When care is pressing you down a bit,
Rest if you must, but please don't quit.

Success is failure turned inside out –
The silver tent of the clouds of doubt,
And you never can tell how close you are,
It may be near when it seems so far –
So stick to the fight when you're hardest hit –
It's when things seem worst, that you mustn't quit.
(AUTHOR UNKNOWN)

SAILSMAN SOLE THEM HALF A MILLION

Report faxed through to the boss by a new salesman, called 'Butch'
"I have scene this outfit, they ain't ever
bort a cent's worth of nothing from us and
I sole them a couple hundred thousand rand's
of guds, I am now going to Beaufort West."

The next fax to the boss by the same man.
"I cum hear and sole them haff a million."

The boss puts the following on the notice board ....
"We ben spending two much time trying to spell
instead of trying to sel. Let's wach thoes sails.
I want everybody should read these faxes from
Booch, who is on the rode doin a grate job for
us, and you should go out and do like he done."
(AUTHOR UNKNOWN)

A SMILE

It costs nothing but means much.
It enriches those who receive it without impoverishing those who give it.
It happens in a flash but the memory sometimes lasts forever.
None are so rich that they can go along without it,
And none so poor but are the richer for its benefits.
It is rest to the weary, daylight to the discouraged,
Sunshine to the sad, and nature's best antidote in time of trouble.
Yes, it cannot be bought, borrowed or stolen,
For it is something that is no earthly use to anyone unless it is given away.
And if in the rush of business, a man is too tired to give you a smile, then leave one of yours,
For no one needs a smile so much as those who have none left to give.
ANONYMOUS

IF YOU ARE UNHAPPY

Once upon a time there was a non-conforming sparrow
who decided not to fly south for the winter.
However, soon after, the weather turned so cold that
he reluctantly started to fly south.
In a short time, ice began to form on his wings and he
fell to earth in a barnyard, almost frozen.

A cow passed by and crapped on the little sparrow.
The sparrow thought it was the end, but the manure
warmed him and defroze his wings, thus, warm and
happy and able to breathe, he started to sing.
Just then a large cat came by and hearing the chirping
investigated the sound.

The cat clawed away the manure, found the chirping
bird and promptly ate him.

This story contains three morals:
1. Everyone who shits on you is not necessarily your enemy.
2. Everyone who gets you out of the shit is not necessarily your friend.
3. And if you are warm and happy in a pile of shit, keep your mouth shut.

ARE YOU A SALESMAN?

If you were
arrested for
being a salesman
would there be
enough evidence
to convict you?

SEE THE PEOPLE

If we were unable to speak ...
There would be nothing.
No ships, no cars, no television,
no aeroplanes, no business, no cities –
if you can't tell it, you can't sell it.

A salesman must see people to tell them about his product.

THE INDISPENSABLE

Sometimes when you're feeling important
Sometimes when your ego's in bloom
Sometimes when you take it for granted
You're the best qualified in the room
Sometimes when you feel that your going
will leave an unfillable hole

SUCCESS TRIVIA

Just follow this simple instruction
and see how it humbles your soul –
Take a bucket and fill it with water
Put your hand in it up to the wrist
Pull it out, and the hole that remains
is a measure of how long you'll be missed.
You may splash all you please when you enter,
You can stir up the water galore –
But stop and you'll find in a minute,
That it looks quite the same as before.

The moral in this quaint example
Is do just the best you can
Be proud of yourself but remember
There's *No Indispensable Man*.

THE SALESMAN

The following modern parable is by James Cahill

And in those days, behold there came through the gates of the city a salesman from afar, and it came to pass as the day went by that he sold plenty.

And in that city were they that were the order takers, spent their days in adding to the alibi sheets. Mightily were they astonished. They said one to the other, "What the hell; how doth he getteth away with it?" And it came to pass that many were gathered in the back office and a soothsayer came among him, saying, "How is it that this stranger accomplished the impossible?"

Whereupon the soothsayer made answer, "He of whom you speak is a hustler. He ariseth very early in the morning and goeth forth full of enthusiasm. He complaineth not, neither doth he know despair. He is arrayed in purple and fine linen, while ye go forth with pants undressed.

"While ye gather here and say one to the other, 'Verily this is a terrible day to work', he is already abroad. And when the eleventh hour cometh, he needeth no alibis. He knoweth his line and they that would stave him off, they give him orders. Men say unto him, 'Nay' when he cometh in, yet when goeth forth he hath their signatures on the line that is dotted.

"He taketh with him the two angels, 'Inspiration' and 'Perspiration', and worketh to beat hell.

Verily I say unto you, go and do likewise."

CHAPTER TWELVE

PETTY TRIVIA

CHAPTER TWELVE

PETTY TRIVIA

GOOD STUFF

There is so much
good in the
worst of us.

And so much bad
in the best
of us.

That it hardly
behooves any
of us

To talk about
the rest
of us.
(AUTHOR UNKNOWN)

IRISH GENERAL CERTIFICATE OF EDUCATION 1998
(Time allowed – seven hours)

1. Who won the second World War?
2. Who came second?
3. What is a Silver Dollar made of?
4. Explain Einstein's theory of Hydrodynamics or write your own name in block letters.

PETTY TRIVIA

5. Spell the following: Dog, Cat, Carrot.
6. What time is News at Ten?
7. Approximately, how many Commandments was Moses given?
8. There have been six kings of England named George. The latest was George the Sixth. Name the other five.
9. Write down the numbers from one to ten. (Marks will be deducted for every number out of sequence).
10. Who invented Stephenson's rocker?
11. What musical instrument does "Phil the Fluter" play?
12. Do you understand Newton's law of gravity? (Answer yes or no).
13. Of what country is Dublin the capital? (Candidates must not write on more than two sides of the paper).
14. Spot the deliberate mistake: An apple a day gathers no moss.
15. Name the odd man out: Seamus O'Toole, Sean O'Flaghorty, Mahatma Gandhi, Patrick Murphy.
16. Name the odd man out: Cardinal Heenan, The Pope, Jack the Ripper, Archbishop of Canterbury.
17. What is a Dunker? (a) A person who dips biscuits in his tea? (b) A contraceptive? (c) A lorry used for motorway construction?
    This question need not be answered by Roman Catholics.
18. Name the winning jockey in the 1975 Greyhound Derby.
19. Who built the Great Pyramids? MacAlpine; Wimpeys; Pharaohs; Thyssons.
20. In the Irish Sheepdog Trials of 1972, how many dogs were found guilty?

N.B. Any candidate found copying will be awarded double marks for displaying initiative.

HEAVEN IS WHERE...

Heaven is where ...
Police are British
Cooks are French
Mechanics are German
Lovers are Italian

And it is all organised by the Swiss

Hell is where...
Police are German
Cooks are British
Mechanics are French
Lovers are Swiss

And it is all organised by the Italians

AFRICAN DEFINITIONS FOR HEALTH TERMS

Artery	The study of paintings
Bacteria	The back door of a cafeteria
Barium	What doctors do when a patient dies
Bowel	A letter like A,E,I,O and U
Caesarean Section	A neighbourhood in Rome
Cat Scan	Searching for Kitty
Cauteries	Make eye contact with a female
Colic	A sheep dog
D & C	Where Washington lived
Dilate	To live long
Enema	Not a friend
Foster	Quicker
Genital	Not Jewish
G.I. Series	Soldier's baseball game
Hangnail	Coat hook
Impotent	Distinguished (well known)
Labour Pain	Getting hurt at work
Medical Staff	A doctor's cane
Morbid	A higher offer
Nitrates	Cheaper than day rates
Node	Being aware of
Outpatient	A person who fainted
Pap Smear	A fatherhood test
Pelvis	A cousin of Elvis'
Postoperative	A letter carrier

Recovery Room — A place to do upholstery
Rectum — Damn near killed him
Sciatic — Attic with a view of the sky
Seizure — Roman Emperor
Tablet — A small table
Terminal Illness — Getting sick at an airport
Tumour — More than one
Urine — Opposite of you're out
Varicose — Nearby
Vein — Conceited

A SURVIVOR'S GUIDE TO SABC TV PRONUNCIATION

Beck — not front
Beds — doves, vultures, etc.
Ben — to set alight
Cut — a small donkey drawn vehicle
Doe — a hinged device for closing a hole in the wall
Errors — districts, e.g. 'ebbon errors'
Feather — Cape Town is feather than Johannesburg
Guddin — where you grow 'kebbi-gees'
Get — a hinged device in a fence
Hair — as opposed to him
Hiss — masculine form of hairs
Itch — as in 'itch and aviary par-sin shall hev wun'
Kennel — army officer
Kettle — cows, etc.
Len — to acquire knowledge
Mick — those who will inherit the earth
Pee pull — more than one par-sin
Phlegm — the benign tip of a candle
Piss — symbolised by white doves
Suffa-ring — as in 'the pee pull are suffa-ring'
Teksi — car for hire, parrot teksi, not a memba of teksi assoseshen
Tocks — negotiations
Weaner — takes all

Wekkas ....they do the wek (are supposed to do the work)
Weld ....the earth

DEAR WHITE FELLA

Dear white fella
Cupla tings you orta no:
Firstly, wen I was born I'm *black*
Wen I grow up, I'm *black*
Wen I get sick, I'm *black*
Wen I go out ina sun, I'm *black*
Wen I'm cold, I'm *black*
And wen I get scared, Jeez, I'm still *black*
And wen I die I'm still *black*...
But you *white* fella, you ...
Wen you born, you *pink*
Wen you grow up, you *white*
Wen you get sick, you *green*
Wen you go out ina sun you go *red*
Wen you git cold, you go *blue*
And wen you scared, you *yellow*
and wen you die you go *purple*...
and you got the cheek to call me *coloured!*

CHAPTER THIRTEEN

COMPANY TRIVIA

CHAPTER THIRTEEN

COMPANY TRIVIA

The company, for most of us, is the stress department in our lives. Great fortunes are made or lost on decisions taken in the workplace. It is here where we learn not only to live our lives to the length, but also to the width. Our abilities develop and grow and when we find ourselves at the end of the rope, we just have to tie a knot, hang on and swing – our dreams are always a few sizes too big so that we can grow into them. Sometimes we have little choice but to take the leap and build our wings on the way down. The trivia in this section will help to relieve some of those tensions and bring a smile to a stress-weary face.

A SECRETARY'S PRAYER

Help me, please, to have a memory of an elephant.
Or at least, one that is three years long.
Let me be able, by some miracle, to do six things at once.
And grant me the ability to answer three telephones simultaneously.

As I frantically type a letter which *must* go today.
Although I know it won't get signed until tomorrow.
Give me, I plead, the knowledge of a university professor
along with my poor Matric Certificate and Secretary's Diploma.
Help me never to lose patience searching for a document which is eventually found on the boss' desk.
Help me acquire second sight so that I may know without being told where the boss is, what he is doing and when he will be back.

COMPANY TRIVIA

Keep my ears clear and alert so I may not fail to hear exactly what the boss is dictating, even though he may blow his nose, suck his pipe or stroll around the office.

Grant me perfect eyesight to read drafts hastily written with a blunt pencil, changed by various persons along the line, and amazingly decorated with arrows, lines, asterisks, etc.

Keep me pleasant at twenty-past-four when urgent work is rushed to me and the boss keeps popping in at 30 second intervals to see if it's done.

And when each year draws to an end, grant me the power to keep my mind off such unimportant things as a bonus or rise, and help to keep the next year's resolution to try to be

A perfect and loyal secretary.

THOUGHT FOR THE DAY

One of our illusions is that the present hour
is not the critical decisive hour.
Write it on your heart
that every day is the best day of the year.

ADVERTISING THAT WORKS

There was once a blind man who
used to beg in a beautiful city park.
He sat there with his hat on the ground
ready to receive any donations. He also
had a sign which read:
I am blind.

One fine morning in early spring,
a man passed by on his way to work. He
bent down, wrote something on the sign
and passed on.

That evening, he passed by again on
his way home.
"How was your day?" he enquired of
the blind man.
"Fantastic", came the reply. "Never done
so well. What did you write on the sign?"
"I added a few words to your sign,
so it read:
'It is spring and I am blind'."

RISK

To laugh is to risk appearing a fool.
To weep is to risk appearing sentimental.
To reach out for another is to risk involvement.
To expose feelings is to risk exposing your true self.
To place your ideas, your dreams before the crowd is to risk their loss.
To love is to risk not being loved in return.
To live is to risk dying.
To hope is to risk despair.
But risks must be taken,
Because the greatest hazard in life is to risk nothing.
He may avoid suffering and sorrow,
But he simply cannot learn, feel, change, love... Live.
Chained by his certitudes, he is a slave.
He has forfeited freedom.
Only a person who risks is free.
There is nothing without risk and
Without risk nothing.

MARK TWAIN'S VIEW

A banker is a person who
lends his umbrella when
the sun shines
but wants it back again
as soon as
it begins to rain.

A man begins cutting his wisdom teeth the moment he bites off more than he can chew.

Life can only be understood backwards. But it must be lived forwards.

Restlessness is discomfort and discomfort is the first necessity of progress. Show me a thoroughly satisfied man and I will show you a failure.

EVERYBODY, SOMEBODY, ANYBODY AND NOBODY

This is a story about people named Everybody, Somebody, Anybody and Nobody. There was an important job to be done and Everybody was sure that Somebody would do it. Anybody could have done it but Nobody did it. Somebody got angry about that because it was Everybody's job. Everybody thought Anybody could do it but Nobody realised that Everybody would not do it. It ended up that Everybody blamed Somebody when Nobody did what Anybody could have done.

CHAPTER THIRTEEN

STAFF ANNOUNCEMENT

Company Vehicles – New South Africa

Due to the perks tax on company cars and the price increase on petrol, all company cars will be replaced by bicycles.

The allocation of bicycles is as follows:

Representatives:	Three-speed with bell
Sales Managers:	Three-speed with bell and pump
Branch Managers:	Ten-speed, one mirror and choice of saddle
Directors:	Ten-speed, two mirrors, plastic raincoat, mud flaps and a choice of metallic colours
Managing Directors:	Tandem bicycle with chauffeur

GUIDE TO SAFE FAX

Q: Do I have to be married to have safe fax?

A: Although married people fax quite often, there are many single people who fax complete strangers every day.

Q: My parents say that they never had fax when they were young and were only allowed to write memos to each other until they were 21. How old do you think someone should be before they can fax?

A: Faxing can be performed at any age, once you have learnt the correct procedures.

Q: If I fax something to myself, will I go blind?

A: Certainly not, as far as we can see.

Q: There is a place on our street where you can go and pay to fax. Is this legal?

A: Yes, many people have no other outlet for their fax drives and must pay a 'professional' when their need to fax becomes too great.

Q: Should a cover always be used for faxing?

A: Unless you are really sure of the one you are faxing, a cover should be used to ensure safe fax.

Q: What happens when I incorrectly do the procedure, and I fax prematurely?

A: Don't panic, many people prematurely fax when they haven't faxed in a long time. Just start over. Most people won't mind if you try again.

Q: I have a personal and a business fax. Can transmissions become mixed up?

A: Being bi-faxual can be confusing, but as long as you use a cover with each one, you won't transmit anything you're not suppose to.

WHAT NOT TO CALL YOUR DOG

Everybody who has a dog calls him Rover or Rex.
I call mine Sex.
Now Sex has been very embarrassing to me. When I went to the City Hall to renew his dog licence, I told the clerk I would like to have a licence for Sex.
He said, "I'd like to have one too".
Then I said, "You don't understand, I've had Sex since I was nine years old".
He said, "You must have been quite a kid!"
When I got married and went on honeymoon, I took the dog with me. I told the motel clerk that I wanted a room for my wife and me, and a special room for Sex. He said that every room in the place was for Sex.
I said, "You don't understand, Sex keeps me awake at night".

The clerk said, "Me too".
One day I entered Sex in a contest, but before the competition began, the dog ran away. Another contestant asked me why I was just standing there looking around. I told him that I had planned to have Sex in the contest. He told me that I should be selling my own tickets.
I said. "But you don't understand, I had hoped to have Sex on TV".
He called me a show-off.
When my wife and I separated, we went to court to fight for custody of the dog.
I said, "Your honour, I had Sex before I was married".
He said, "Me too".
Then I told him that after I was married, Sex left me.
He said, "Me too".
Last night Sex ran off again. I spent hours looking around town for him. A cop came to me and asks, "What are you doing in this alley at four o'clock in the morning?"
I said, I'm looking for Sex."

My case comes up on Friday!

WHICH ARE YOU?

Some members keep a group so strong,
While others join just to belong.
Some dig right in; serve with pride;
Some go along just for the ride.

Some volunteer to do their share,
While some lie back and just don't care.
Some do their best, some help, some make;
Some do nothing, only take.

Some greet new members with a smile,
And make their coming so worthwhile,
While some go on their merry way,
No greeting or kind word to say.

Some help the group to grow and grow,
When asked to help they don't say "No".
Some drag, some pull, some don't, some do
Consider, which of these are you?

POLITICAL PHILOSOPHIES

Socialism:	You have two cows and give one to your neighbour.
Communism:	You have two cows. The Government takes both and gives you the milk.
Fascism:	You have two cows. The Government takes both and sells you the milk.
Nazism:	You have two cows. The Government takes both and shoots you.
Great society:	You have two cows. The Government takes both, shoots one, milks the other and throws the milk away.
Capitalism:	You have two cows. You sell one and buy a bull.

DIFFERENT KINDS OF BUYERS

Animal buyer	He will "bear" you in mind
Barber buyer	He wants to "shave" your price
Blanket buyer	He wants you to "cover" him
Blind buyer	He can't "see" it
Card playing buyer	He wants to "pass" on it
Constipated	He first must "unload" what he has
Romantic buyer	He would "love" to buy from you
Musical buyer	He makes a "note" of it
Religious buyer	He wants his boss' "blessings"
Sexy buyer	He wants to "sleep" on it
Real buyer	He looks, he likes and he buys

ANSWER ME: Ladies and gentlemen, the basic questions that need to be answered today are:

Where have we come from?
How did we get here?
What are we doing here?
Where are we going to?
How are we going to get there?
And what the hell are we going to do when we get there?

MEN ARE FOUR

He who knows not, and knows not he knows not
he is a fool, shun him.
He who knows not, and knows he knows not,
he is simple, teach him.
He who knows and knows not he knows
he is asleep, wake him.
He who knows, and knows he knows
he is wise, follow him.

THE WHY CHECK-LIST

1. Why move along with the stream?
2. Why be like a windmill, always turning with the wind?
3. Why not think for yourself?
4. Why not stand up for what is right?
5. Why not believe in yourself and your mission?
6. Why retreat from a mistake?
7. Why not tackle the big idea?
8. Why not be prepared, be equipped and be capable?

After all, you are unique and very special. With hundreds of bones in your body, 72 miles of nerve tissue, your heart beats 30 000 times every year, pumps 70 000 litres of blood every five years and you have a rustproof, waterproof covering. Why not? Go for it!

REAL ESTATE

Remember these words of famous men...

The big fortunes of the future will be made in land.
JOHN D. ROCKEFELLER

Every person who invests in land near a growing city,
adopts the surest and safest
method of becoming independent,
for land is the basis of wealth.
THEODORE ROOSEVELT

"Land cannot be stolen, nor can it be carried away.
Purchased with common sense,
it is about the safest investment in the world."
FRANKLIN D. ROOSEVELT

"Buying land is not only the best way,
the quickest way, and the safest way, but the only way
to become wealthy."
MARSHAL FIELD

"Buy on the fringe and wait. Hold what you buy."
JOHN JACOB ASTOR

"Land is an imperishable asset, ever increasing in value.
It is the most solid security that human ingenuity
has devised and about the only indestructible security."
RUSSEL SAGE

"No investment on earth is so safe, so sure, so certain
to enrich its owner as undeveloped land.
Place your savings in land near a growing city – there is no such
savings bank anywhere."
GROVER CLEVELAND

CHAPTER THIRTEEN

WORKING DAYS IN THE NEW SOUTH AFRICA

Believe it or not, there's just no time.
Would you believe everyone spends the whole year lolling around in idleness? Here's the proof:

Every year has	365 days
If you sleep eight hours/day	122 days
This leaves	243 days
If you rest eight hours/day	122 days
This leaves	121 days
You certainly don't work on Sundays	52 days
This leaves	69 days
Everyone takes a half day on Saturday	26 days
This leaves	43 days
If you take one and a half hours for lunch and tea	28 days
This leaves	15 days
Everyone must take at least two weeks vacation	14 days
This leaves	1 day
This one day is Labour Day when simply nobody works	1 day
So you can see that you have left for work	0 days

A GREAT MAN MUST BE MINDFUL OF NINE THINGS:

- To see beyond where he looks
- To listen beyond what he hears
- To be gentle in looks
- To be respectful in manners
- To be true to his words
- To take pride in his works
- To ask when in doubt
- To think of the consequences when in anger
- To think of justice and fairness when accepting an advantage

Confucius (551 – 479 BC)

CHAPTER FOURTEEN

PRESENTATION SPEECH

CHAPTER FOURTEEN

PRESENTATION SPEECH

Ladies and Gentlemen

The idea that all men are brothers has influenced the actions of mankind for at least 2 000 years. In one sense every world religion is an organisation for brotherhood. To some extent this can also be said of ours, because we bring together those who are concerned with promoting the high ideals and professional skills. The concept of brotherhood is however not confined to sharing one's ideals and skill, but also to develop the right attitude and enthusiasm with which to approach our very demanding careers.

As a body of men and women who share a common interest, we represent a respected pressure group while also being a responsible opinion former. We make up the hard core of people upon whom so many communities rely.

We attract factories and businesses to our cities and towns that provide employment and security to our fellow human beings, but most of all... our objective is to serve our members. We serve them in many different ways which enhance their opportunity to grow to their fullest ability... that is what our institute is all about. However, the immediate occasion for bringing us together tonight is to pay tribute to one of the best loved estate agents in South Africa, one of the doyens of professional real estate practice – we have with us tonight a man who, with the help of others like him, fathered the Estate Agents Board – spawned the articles of association that today serve as the constitution of our Institute and used the collective negotiating power of our mem-

PRESENTATION SPEECH

bers to influence legislation that has brought order and integrity to our young profession.

We are gathered here tonight amongst other things to say thanks you to one of our members, for a job well-done. His unbridled enthusiasm has changed the lives of many men and women in our ranks for the better and he has made our job of being estate agents more worthwhile.

For his service to us, there were no rewards demanded – nor were any ever given. He was content with making advances in the field of education, legislation and with the spiritual fulfilment that comes from the love of your fellowmen. In these difficult days, it is nice to know that we have around us a man that radiates so much confidence, who sponsored a harmony of purpose unrivaled in other institutes. A man who was able to co-ordinate our combined strength into a more satisfactory career for all of us – a man called Trevor Randall.

It is men like Trevor who have taught us how to become a respected pressure group and responsible opinion formers. Our institute must maintain a high profile and continue to build upon the progress of the past. Commitment is an essential role in the overall development of our young profession. The creation of wealth amongst all South Africans is vital to the advancement of our social and economic standards – at the forefront of our priorities should be property ownership.

Our Institute's objectives were formulated by men like Trevor who devoted the best part of his life towards achieving this end. Our Institute has become the accepted voice of estate agents throughout South Africa – it is through men like him that our Institute has grown in influence and stature – our Institute would not have been established, nor would it have withstood the test of nearly 60 years of service if it had not been for the commitment of experienced real estate practitioners like him. I came across the following passage in the minutes of the 18th AGM held at the Culemborg, Pretoria, in 1955.

"Under all is land, upon its wise utilisation and widely allocated ownership, depends the survival and the growth of our civilisation. The estate agent is the instrument through which the land resource of a country reaches its highest and best use and through which land ownership attains its highest distribution. The estate agent is a creator of homes, a builder of cities, a developer of industries and of productive farms. Such functions impose obligations beyond those of ordinary commerce, they impose a grave social responsibility and a patriotic duty to which the estate agent is dedicated and for which he diligently prepares himself. The estate agent is dedicated to maintaining and improving the standards of his calling and shares with his fellow estate agents a common responsibility for its integrity and its honour!"

I could think of no better description of Trevor Randall than that:

I am proud that you have called upon me to present this leather-bound personalised copy of our real estate sales guide to Trevor, because as president of the Institute of Realtors of South Africa, I can think of no more pleasurable thing to do than to be here and to ask him to step forward and accept this special copy of our very first publication. With this presentation copy of the real estate sales guide goes our best wishes for a great future, a long and happy life and our thanks for your unselfish hard work in the past.

CHAPTER FIFTEEN

AFTER DINNER

CHAPTER FIFTEEN

AFTER DINNER

Ladies and gentlemen, we are not gathered here this evening for a display of virtuosity, but to have some fun. Give me my golf clubs, fresh air and a beautiful partner, and *you can keep the golf clubs and the fresh air*. A stunning blond walked into a pro shop, and asked the pro:
"I wonder if I might try on that golf blouse in the window?"
"Go right ahead", he replied, "it might help business."

I went down to the Royal Natal National Park in the Drakensberg mountains for a weekend. On arrival I asked the clerk at the check-in counter:
"Where's the golf course?"
"There isn't one", he said.
"What, no golf course, what are people supposed to do around here, *look at the scenery?*"

The greatest golfing character in my family is my mother-in-law, Lammie. Whenever I play with old Lammie we have a very speedy round together because she doesn't worry about the players ahead of us. On every fairway we come to, the four balls ahead hide in the bushes until she passes them by. She's the only golfer I know who has to shout "*fore!*" when she putts. Old Lammie is quite a girl! She claims that at 80 she can still do all the things today that she used to do at 18! It just goes to show how useless she must have been at eighteen. I offered to send her on holiday to the Valley of a Thousand Hills with all expenses paid! The only condition was that she had to spend *a year on each hill...* she refused! She must have been quite a stunner at 18, they tell me she was 36" 22" 36" *and that was only her left leg.*

167

AFTER DINNER

Golf is getting too tough for me these days and I'm seriously thinking of giving it up. I walked in the locker room at Waterkloof Country Club the other day and there they've got steel wire brushes labelled "to scrub your balls". Besides that, I now find that even though I can afford to lose a couple of balls these days, I haven't got the strength to hit them away.

We should never speak so that people understand us... we should speak so that they don't misunderstand us.

A friend of mine had a flat wheel on the highway between Pretoria and Johannesburg the other day. After changing the wheel, he discovered that his battery was flat... he was unable on his own to push the car fast enough to start it, because it was an automatic. After about a half hour, he managed to flag down a young serviceman who had just got his army driver's licence the week before. The young man was most emphatic that he was not allowed to use a military vehicle for anything but military purposes. My friend explained to him that he was in fact an off duty Brigadier and that by coincidence he knew the commanding officer in charge of the serviceman's transport unit.

"OK", said the young soldier. "I'll do it, but I have never pushed a car in my life before." The Brigadier assured him there that there was nothing to it and after lining the bumpers up to make sure it would work, he explained to the youngster that because his car was automatic, he would have to push him at a speed of at least 60 km/h or else his engine would not start. After a long wait in the car and wondering when the youngster was going to do something... he looked into the rear view mirror and, sure enough, there he was 40 meters away and approaching at exactly 60 km/h.

According to statistics, you are going to forget 48% of what I have told you by tomorrow afternoon this time, 86% within two weeks. In a month's time, you will have forgotten 99,5 % of what I have said to you today.

Memory is a wonderful thing. If you think you have a good memory, you will have one. If you think you don't, you won't.

CHAPTER FIFTEEN

I bought a book on memory training and never use it! I put it down somewhere and forgot where I put it.

I met a fellow in America. He does his shopping differently – buys everything he needs through mail order from Sears. Even ordered a vasectomy through Sears – works fine – every time a pretty girl walks past his house the garage doors open up.

You get two kinds of people in life:
- those who think they can; and
- those who think they can't

The interesting thing is that they are both right. When I first discovered this wonderful truth. I thought that I had better think that I am something good, so I thought that I should be a consultant.

I'm sure you all know what a consultant is:
- Someone who knows 60 different ways of making love, but he doesn't have a girlfriend.
- I had a tomcat once. He used to cause havoc around our neighbourhood. I took him to the vet and had him fixed... *now he's a consultant too.*
  Things are never going to be the same again!

At Loftus Versfeld we have a fireworks display every year. Last year the fellow who puts it on for charity made it known that this was going to be the biggest and the best ever. The stadium was packed to capacity... *and he lit the wrong fuse!*

Well, a sky-rocket went up his trouser leg, set his underpants on fire and what a commotion. The next morning my wife saw him on crutches at the Brooklyn Shopping Mall. She walked up to him and said, "But aren't you the same man that puts on the fireworks display at Loftus?"
He said, "No, ma'am, and I never will be again!"

While at the shopping mall, my wife bought a book on jogging for R25, then she bought jogging shoes for R80, a tracksuit for R90, joined a jogging club for R45 – now I know what they mean when they say, my wife is running into debt.

Talking to my Bank Manager about a mutual acquaintance, he said, "Yes, old Harry has also gone to that eternal resting place."
I said: "What! I didn't even know old Harry had died."
He said:,"I didn't say he died!... *He now works for the government.*"

My secretary got me into a lot of trouble a little while ago, she had laddered her stocking for the umpteenth time on a screw protruding from my desk. She protested angrily and asked me when I would have my desk repaired. I said sympathetically, "Please take some money from the petty cash and replace your stockings, I will have my desk attended to as soon as I can. When the auditors arrived they wanted an explanation from me for an entry in the Petty Cash Book "for screw on desk – R75".

Yes, I suppose we would all still have been living in Paradise if it were not for women. Picture old Adam for a moment saying, "We had peaches, plums, pears, avocadoes, pineapples, almost anything she could possibly want, *but no, she had to have an apple!*

This reminds me that you get two different kinds of people at every party – those who want to go home early – and those who want to stay to the end. Unfortunately, they are usually married to each other.

I suppose that this brings us to the question, "What is a wife?" Well, it's someone who helps you through those difficult situations that you would never have got into *if you hadn't got married!*

My wife was mugged in Johannesburg recently. They stole her handbag with all her credit cards in it... I haven't reported it to the police yet because the thief is spending far less than my wife with her credit cards.

Driving through the Kruger Park, my son asked me, "Do monkeys get married, Dad?"
I said, "Only monkeys get married!"

CHAPTER FIFTEEN

SAY IT WITH FLOWERS

A friend of mine died and at the same time I had just signed up a lease agreement with a large government department. I decided to express my feelings by sending flowers. The florist shop got the messages mixed up and at the funeral that day there was a beautiful wreath with a message 'Enjoy your new accommodation', and the government department got a lovely vase of flowers with the message 'Rest in peace'. Later on I wanted to impress a rather attractive young lady in town so I sent her two dozen red roses with a message, 'To the most beautiful girl in town, one rose for every year of your life'. I couldn't understand why she never phoned to thank me and went to the florist to find out if they had sent the flowers. "Oh yes, and after the last mix up the manager decided to put in an extra two dozen roses with our compliments, sir."

A young apprentice plumber, realising that the country was on the brink of enormous changes and that communication would play a vital role in his future, decided to go to university to study languages. But like most youngsters, he had no money. So he asked his father to keep him at university. His father was a hardened man without much education or money... who said, "I'm not paying for you at university *until you know what's what!*"

Despondent, he went to the neighbourhood pub and had a few beers. While sitting there drinking, one of the local girls came over to him and asked him, "Why are you drinking so much?" He told her his sad story whereupon she invited him to come over to her flat for coffee. After a short while, she slipped into the bathroom and came out a few minutes later wearing only a see-through negligè. He looked up and seeing her pubic hair through the sexy garment said, "Hey, what's that?"
She looked down and asked, *"What's what?"*
He said, *"If I knew* that my dad would pay for me at university!"

With all these opportunities going around we need a happy healthy middle-aged life. *We all* want a happy healthy middle-aged life, *don't we?* A friend of mine says he's found it. For that happy medium he takes

171

Salusa 45 on Mondays, Tuesdays and Wednesdays and baths in Staysoft on Thursdays and Fridays. But watch out, he warns for Salusa 95... that stuff is so potent, you need a tyre lever to get your underpants on in the mornings.

In closing, they say that good wives laugh at their husbands' jokes – if that is true then we have a lot of good wives present here tonight because I am sure that you have heard all these stories from your husbands before. Thank you for laughing.

CHAPTER SIXTEEN

WEDDINGS

CHAPTER SIXTEEN

WEDDINGS

Wedding ceremonies are occasions that I have very strong views on. Too often a beautiful day is spoiled by an inconsiderate master of ceremonies who tells off-colour stories and ruins what could have been a wonderful day. Without being too prescriptive, I have selected material that could be used on this memorable day for proposing toasts to the bridal couple and the parents. Also included are suitable jokes that can be told in public on the wedding day. Remember that the bride's heart is overflowing with happiness, the relatives and friends have come from afar to share it with the couple. She is filled with emotion and prays that she has made the right choice, she wants to cherish the memory for the rest of her life and hopes that each anniversary will reinforce her love for him. She wants to be his darling forever. She seeks only God's blessings and your good wishes that her calling as a wife and later on as a mother will be fulfiled.

The bridegroom has won the most precious prize that any man could ever want, the heart of his beautiful bride. On this day he makes a vow, a covenant with God, to love her, protect her and honour her until death them do part. Why spoil it with objectionable garbage?

AN OLD INDIAN LEGEND

When woman was conceived, the Creator used the following ingredients:

The fullness of the moon and the adaptability of a young vine, the rustle of grass when in seed and the fragile form of a slender reed, the blossom of a tree in springtime and the delicate touch of a newly formed leaf, the transparency of a sunbeam and some tears from a cloud, the variable nature of the wind and the nervousness of a fawn, the immortality of a peacock and the vulnerability of down from a new born chick, the resilience of a diamond and the sweetness of honey, the ruthlessness of a tiger and the glowing warmth from a fire, the numbing chill from glacial snow and the talkativeness of a parrot, the voice of a nightingale, the deviousness of a snake and the devotion of a lioness towards her cubs.

The Creator then gave this woman to man. After a week, man returned to the Creator and said, "This woman is making my life miserable. She talks incessantly and interferes with me all the time. Because of this I don't get any rest for my soul anymore. She says that I don't pay her enough attention and demands more and more of my time. She cries over the silliest things, yet while at home she lives in comfort. I want to give her back to you." The Creator was obliged to take her back but after a week man was back again.

This time he pleads, "My life seems so empty now, I think of her all the time, I just can't get her out of my mind, I miss her dearly, when I think of how she used to dance and sing, the way she used to look into my eyes and talk to me. The way she snuggled up to me, she was so beautiful to look at and so soft and tender to touch. Her laughter was like music to my ears, her presence brought calmness into my heart, please give her back to me."

The Creator did so immediately. Three days later man was back again, this time he said, "Lord, I beg of you take her back, she gives me more problems than pleasure." Then, without hesitation, he says, "I can't live with her, but by the same token I can't live without her either. Oh, what shall I do?"

"Lord, please give me the knowledge to understand her, for if I understand her, I shall be able to understand everything in life."

GENESIS 2: 18 – 24

So from the soil, the Lord fashioned all the wild beasts and all the birds of heaven. These he brought to the man to see what he would call them; each one would bear the name the man would give it.

The man gave names to all the cattle, all the birds of heaven and all the wild beasts. But no helpmate suitable for man was found for him. So the Lord God made the man fall into a deep sleep, and while he slept, he took one of his ribs and enclosed it in flesh. The Lord God built the rib he had taken from the man into a woman, and brought her to the man.

The man exclaimed, "This at last is bone from my bones and flesh from my flesh! This is to be called Woman, for this was taken from man. This is why man leaves his father and mother and joins himself to his wife, and they become one body."

THE FIRST LETTER OF ST. PAUL TO THE CORINTHIANS:

Be ambitious for the higher gifts. And I am going to show a way that is better than any of them.

If I have all the eloquence of men or of angels, but speak without love, I am simply a gong booming or a cymbal clashing. If I have the gifts of prophecy, understanding all the mysteries there are, and knowing everything, and if I have faith in all its fullness, to move mountains, but without love, then I am nothing at all. If I give away all that I possess, piece by piece, and if I even let them take my body to burn it, but am without love, it will do me no good whatever.

Love is always patient and kind; it is never jealous; love is never boastful or conceited; it is never rude or selfish; it does not take offence, and is not resentful. Love takes no pleasure in other people's sins but delights in the truth; it is always ready to excuse, to trust, to hope, and to endure whatever comes. Love does not come to an end.

THE LORD'S COMMANDMENT

This is the word of the Lord and the Lord said to his disciples, "This is my commandment:

Love one another, as I have loved you. A man can have no greater love than to lay down his life for his friends. You are my friends. If you do what I command you, I shall not call you servants anymore, because a servant does not know his master's business; I call you friends, because I have made known to you everything I have learnt from my Father. You did not choose me, no, I chose you; and I commissioned you to go out and to bear fruit, fruit that will last; and then the Father will give you anything you ask him in my name."

CLIMATE CLASH

He takes off a sweater
I put one more on.
He kicks off the blanket
I'm frozen to dawn.

He opens a window
I turn up the heat
He walks around barefoot
I've woollen-clad feet.

But we love each other.
Ecstatically,
though not attuned,
thermostatically!
(AUTHOR UNKNOWN)

THE ART OF MARRIAGE

A good marriage must be created
In the marriage the little things are the big things
It is never being too old to hold hands
It is remembering to say "I love you" at least once a day
It is never going to sleep angry
It is having a mutual sense of values and common objectives
It is standing together and facing the world
It is forming a circle of love that gathers in the whole family
It is speaking words of appreciation and demonstrating gratitude in thoughtful ways
It is having a capacity to forgive and forget
It is giving each other an atmosphere in which each can grow
It is a common search for the good and the beautiful
It is not only marrying the right person, it is being the right partner.

THE MARRIAGE CHECK LIST

1. Give credit where credit is due
2. Both partners must participate in planning
3. Gain each other's confidence
4. Listen to one another's proposals
5. If one's behaviour is unusual, find out why
6. Make your wishes known by suggestion
7. Admit mistakes
8. Criticize constructively
9. Set the example
10. Be consistent
11. Settle strife immediately
12. Back up your partner

A good marriage creates success and success causes:
(a) Growth
(b) Change
(c) Crisis

(d) Crisis requires solutions
(e) Solutions result in success

What's the pay-off?

If you find time, you make love!

NOTHING SUITED HIM

He sat at the dinner table there, with
discontented frown,
the potatoes and steak were underdone
and the bread was baked too brown,
the pie was sour, the pudding too sweet,
and the mincemeat much too fat.
The soup was greasy too and salty,
'twas hardly fit for a cat.

"I wish you could taste the bread and
pies I have seen my mother bake,
they were something like and 'twould
do you good;
just to look at a slice of her cake."

Said the smiling wife, "I'll improve
with age,
just now I'm a beginner,
but your mother called to see me
today and I got *her* to cook the dinner.
(AUTHOR UNKOWN)

TOAST TO THE PARENTS OF THE BRIDE

George and Drien have always struck me as being people with enough of everything, not too much, not too little, just enough.

Enough good health to make their work load a pleasure.
Enough success to provide their children with all their fondest wants, hopes and desires.
Enough strength to overcome all their problems.
Enough patience to carry on until they win.
Enough love, they must have enough love because they share it with their friends and family.
Enough religion to make God a reality and not just a name in their lives.
Enough hope to tackle the future with pride and confidence.

Ladies and gentlemen, *I have said enough*, will you please stand and drink with me a toast to George and Drien.

TOAST TO THE PARENTS OF THE GROOM

It is indeed an honour to be called upon to propose a toast to a couple who have been on honeymoon for the past 35 years. Yes, they have found a recipe that works. I would like to give you that recipe as I see it and I know them well.

Buckets full of love
Heaps of thanks
A container of kind deeds
Tons of loyalty
Mounds of good thoughts
A valley full of tenderness
Mountains of hope
Lots and lots of compassion

Mix thoroughly, adding a few tears of joy, sorrow and sympathy for others. Flavour with gifts of friendship, love and service. Fold in sufficient faith to lighten the other ingredients and raise them to a texture of great heights of living. Bake well at a high degree of human kindness and with warm smiles, serve generously.

That, ladies and gentlemen is how I see my dear friends, Gert and Edna. Please stand now and drink a toast to a really fine couple. To Gert and Edna.

TOAST TO THE BRIDE AND GROOM

Marriages are created in heaven. There can be no doubt about that. On this happy occasion we celebrate the day that Peter and Burnette promised each other their undying love. It may just be appropriate to remind them at this stage that thunderstorms are also created in heaven.

I have been an eyewitness to their beautiful love story and have watched with great pleasure the tenderness, the love and the caring nature that has developed from their relationship. This was one courtship that all of us who are close to them knew would culminate in marriage. I can now understand why people say that when two people get married they become one, even if they have the occasional tiff to decide which one.

I know that Peter will treasure her love as his most precious possession. I also know that Burnette has conquered the most eligible bachelor in town and, as she tenderly looks after, him will make him feel like a king.

They have been a wonderful young couple and they will become respected parents and leading citizens in our community. They say that marriage is out of fashion these days, well, if that is so, then I have never seen a bridal couple looking so happy to be out of fashion.

Ladies and gentlemen, please rise ... as we drink a toast to Peter and Burnette!

THE BEST MAN'S SPEECH AT A WEDDING

Tradition has it that if something happens to the bridegroom on the way to church, then the best man steps into his shoes and marries the bride. What an absolute pleasure that would be, looking at this beautiful bride,

I think that Arthur is very fortunate that that custom is not practised anymore... because then I might have arranged for something to happen to him.

Wedding days are meant to be unforgettable and I know that this one will certainly be. Did you see how happy Arthur and Karen looked while making their vows to each other in church this afternoon? It convinced me that this love affair is going to last. Look at them now and you'll see what two people who are deeply *in love*, look like.

Arthur and Karen have been good friends of mine for many years. In fact, I introduced them to one another. This more than anything else, makes their wedding day a very special day for me as well, and I know that you will all agree with me when I say that they are the perfect match.

Please rise to this occasion and drink a toast to Arthur and Karen.

THE BRIDEGROOM

The bridegroom at most weddings seems to get heckled, interrupted and shouted down – for some reason it has become a culture to put him into an awkward spot. If you are prepared for it, you will certainly win the day. One way of putting noisy guests in their place is by saying something like this:

"I have heard that the guests who make a lot of noise at weddings usually bring the smallest presents." If that doesn't work then just simply allow them the time to sing or make interruptions as you go along, they will soon settle down.

THE SPEECH

"First of all, I would like to thank Mary for consenting to marry me – I must be the luckiest man on earth... doesn't she look absolutely beautiful?

"Next, I would like to thank my new *mom* and *dad* for accepting me into their family. Don't worry, I will take good care of her. I would also like to thank my own parents for everything they have done for me and for the way that they have accepted Mary as a daughter. Even though I had no choice – I have got the best parents in the world." (If any grandparents are present, special mention is made of them.)

"Having dispensed with the most important part of my speech please allow me to also thank the vicar for the wonderful service – it was really very special and it made Mary and I feel very close to God when we made our vows; and a special thanks to all our wonderful friends and family who have travelled great distances to be with us today."

(Thereafter the usual thanks: – to the creators of the wedding gown, the wedding cake, the flowers, etc., etc.)

Last but not least, the bridesmaids, the best man (the driver of the bridal car) and our wonderful master of ceremonies.

TRANSLATED FROM A.G. VISSER

Marriage follows in the footsteps of love
In a fragrance of roses sent from above

But who spares a thought while
imbibing in wine
For the hangover that follows
when you need to feel fine.

A BRIDE'S PRAYER

Heavenly Father, I am so happy I am almost afraid. I pray that the serenity of this day will never be dulled, but that it will grow more beautiful with each passing year. Help us to create a climate in our hearts that will make our love grow so strong that it will not falter through a single failure. Give us enough time together so that we can develop a truly mature love, a love that will grow like a tree, growing slowly from a seed in the ground to the sheltering splendour of its prime.

Lord, bless our love with honesty of the heart so that we can share what is genuine within ourselves. Help us to understand that it is foolish to expect perfection, and please give us the courage to accept one another as we are. Make us the instruments of your love so that we can radiate your message so brightly that others will follow in that light. Father, thank you for making this day the happiest day of my life.

Amen.

CHAPTER SEVENTEEN

JOKES

JOKES

NEVER LOSE YOUR HEAD FOR A BIT OF FLUFF

A little worm lived alongside the railway track and every day he used to crawl along the railway line and position himself next to the points. He was fascinated by the way the points would snap, open and close again to change the tracks of the passing trains.

One day he was sitting on top of the railway line when the points snapped closed and nipped off the fluff at the end of his tail. He went home crying. His mother comforted him saying, "Don't worry my little worm, go back and fetch your fluff, and mommy will sew it back on for you."

So, happily, he crawled back and while sitting on top of the railway line again, he leaned over to reach for his fluff when the points snapped closed once more and off went his head.

The moral of this little story is... you should never lose your head for a bit of fluff.

DOCTOR

A doctor phones a plumber and asks him to come over because his drain is blocked. Upon arrival, the plumber wants a R60 house call charge. The doctor complains and says to the plumber, "I spent seven years at

university to become a doctor and all I get for a house call is R30."
"I know" said the plumber, "that's all I used to get when I was a doctor too!"

PISTOL WHISTLE

The bride's uncle had to travel a dusty and rather remote road through the Free State to get to the wedding. On arrival in town he booked into the local hotel to have a shower and a change of clothing. After the wedding and on his way back home, he remembered that he had left his 9 mm pistol in the hotel room.

He made an about-turn and upon arrival back at the hotel he went straight to the room. Unbeknown to him, the bridal couple had checked into the same room that he had occupied earlier that afternoon and as he opened the door, this is what he heard:

"Whose little nosey posey is this?"
"It's your's, my sweetheart."
"And whose little chinny chin chin is this?"
"It's also yours, my sweetie pie."
"And whose little earsy pearsys are these?"
"They're yours, my darling, tonight *everything is yours.*"
At that point, the uncle interjected and said, "Now look here, when you two get to that little *pistol whistle*, it's mine, you understand?!"

DIFFERENT GENERATIONS

An old-fashioned grandmother had a wonderful relationship with her teenage granddaughter. The teenager was into computers, the ozone layer and all sorts of modern-day concepts that Granny had never understood.

One day they were having a shower together and Granny finished first. After drying herself, she took a can of aerosol deodorant from the shelf and started spraying it underarm. The granddaughter, shocked, said in a raised voice, "Granny, what about the hole in the ozone layer?" "Oh, don't worry about that honey, I'll just give it a good wipe with the face cloth."

STOP DRINKING

My doctor says I should stop drinking and eating expensive food – it will help me to pay his account.

MISTAKES

"Doctor, have you ever made a mistake?"
"Yes, I once took a man's tonsils out and only later found out that he could afford an appendectomy."

WHAT'S WRONG?

"Did the doctor ever find out what you had?" "Almost ... I had R100 and he charged R90."

DROP YOUR PANTS

When a bridegroom was doing his housemanship, he went to the X-ray department where there was a rather attractive young radiologist on duty. A country bumpkin had come in for a chest X-ray and was standing in front of the X-ray machine. When the bridegroom noticed that he was wearing a pair of pants with a large belt and metal buckle, he looked at the man and said, "Drop your pants!" Whereupon the man crouched behind the screen.
"Drop your pants" he said again. The man crouched a little more, and he then walked up to the man and asked, "Do you understand English?"
"Yes, of course" he said.
"Well, then drop your pants."
"Oh, sorry" said the country bumpkin, "I thought you were talking to the radiologist."

IT DOESN'T MATTER WHERE YOU HIDE IT

Abie had got married to Rebecca and on the first night she was very shy. So she asked Abie to go for a walk around the block while she took a bath and got herself ready. Being a considerate man, Abie agreed and went for a walk. When he returned, he knocked at the door.
Rebecca asked, "Who is it?"
Abie replied, "It's me, Beckie."
She said, "I'm not ready yet, please walk some more."
OK" said Abie and off he went again.
The next time, he knocked and Rebecca asked, "Who is it?"
He replied, "It's me, Abie."
She said, "I'm not ready yet, please walk again."
This time, Abie was a little disappointed and decided to peep through the keyhole. He saw Beckie sitting in front of the mirror with a powder puff in one hand and puffing under first one armpit and then the other. He looked at this for a while and said through the keyhole, "Beckie, it doesn't matter where you hide it, I'll still find it!"

VETERINARY SCIENCE

A young lady wanted to be a vet but the professors were reluctant to accept her, saying that at Onderstepoort they call a spade a spade and that it might embarrass a young lady. She replied that as the only daughter in a family of eight, there was nothing she had not heard before. She was accepted.

One day, the professor wanted to demonstrate how to extract sperm from a bull which would then be used for artificial insemination. All the students were gathered around, but try as the professor might, the bull stubbornly refused to give sperm. Eventually the professor, quite exhausted, grabbed the bull by the hair between the horns and shook his head vigorously. Suddenly, the bull performed and did all that was required of him.

The young lady started laughing uncontrollably. The professor was quite annoyed and asked the young lady what she found so funny about this very scientific demonstration. She eventually stopped laughing and apologised to the professor saying, "I always wondered where all the bald men came from."

BANK MANAGERS

During my last visit to my bank manager, he said, "Please sit down." I replied, "I'm quite comfortable on my knees, thank you."

He said to me, "If you can prove to me that you don't need the money and bring me two people to sign as sureties, I will lend it to you."

In the old country people would not lend me money because they knew me – here they won't lend me money because they don't know me.

My bank manager said, "We've done more for you than even your own mother – we've carried you for 12 months."

KISS YOUR MOTHER-IN-LAW

The bridegroom's future mother-in-law had an accident and her face was badly mutilated. She had to have a skingraft and asked the surgeon to take skin from her buttocks.

He was interested in this request and asked, "Why from your buttocks?" She said, "Whenever my son-in-law comes to visit it will give me pleasure turning that side of my face to him when he kisses me."

CONSTRUCTION MAN

In October, a construction man said to his seven-year-old daughter that she could have anything her heart desired for Christmas. She discussed this very enthusiastically with her mother and then out of the blue decided that she wanted a baby brother. The mother was quite surprised and said to her daughter, "That's impossible!"
"Why?" the seven-year-old wanted to know.
"Well, my darling, it's already October and Christmas is less than three months away. Your daddy can't make you a baby brother in that time."
"Yes, he can" said the little mite, "he'll just have to put more men on the job."

LAWYERS

A lawyer dies and goes to heaven. As the lawyer passes through the Pearly Gates, a crowd is waiting and cheering. The lawyer is amazed at the reception and sees St. Peter in front of the crowd. "A special day" St. Peter proclaims. "It's not every day that we get the opportunity to welcome someone here who has lived for 145 years."

"Uh, 145?" the lawyer muses aloud. "But I was only 59 when I passed away."

St. Peter looks concerned. "What is the meaning of this!" he exclaims. "Summon the Holy Accountant at once!"

Very soon a brown-suited angel appears, peering through bi-focals and frantically flipping through the pages of a very large ledger. "I don't understand where I could have made a mistake" the Holy Accountant says, "I added up his billable hours..."

A lawyer and an accountant are sitting next to each other on a long flight from England. The lawyer leans over to the accountant and asks if he would like to play a fun game. The accountant just wants to take a nap so politely declines. The lawyer persists and explains that the game is really easy and a lot of fun. He explains, "I ask you a question and if you don't know the answer, you pay me R5." Again the accountant declines and tries to get some sleep. The lawyer, now somewhat agitated, says, "OK, if you don't know the answer you pay me R5 and if I don't know the answer, I'll pay you R50." This catches the accountant's complete attention and he agrees to play the game.

The lawyer asks the first question. "What's the distance from the earth to the moon?" The accountant doesn't say a word, reaches into his wallet, pulls out R5 and hands it to the lawyer. Now it's the accountants turn. He asks the lawyer: "What goes up a hill with three legs, and comes down with four?" The lawyer looks at him with a puzzled look. He takes out his laptop and searches all his references. He taps into the air phone with his modem and searches the Net. Frustrated, he sends e-mails to all his co-workers and friends he knows. All to no avail. After an hour, he wakes the accountant and hands him R50. The accountant politely takes the money and tries to go back to sleep. The lawyer, more than a little miffed, shakes the accountant and asks, "Well, so what is the answer?" Without saying a word, the accountant reached into his wallet, hands the lawyer R5 and goes back to sleep.

HAPPILY MARRIED

I have been happily married for 20 years – never been unhappy! Thank goodness for that because my happy years were *hell on earth.*

LEAD IN HIS PENCIL

Mike went into a pub for a beer. He saw the barman pour a beer into a tankard then added milk and a raw egg, stirred it up and drank it down. Mike asked, "How can you drink that stuff?"
The barman replied, "First of all, it has nothing to do with you, secondly, I like it, and thirdly, it puts lead in my pencil."

Mike was most impressed with that answer and the next time Kallie came to visit, Mike mixed one of those cocktails, stirred it up and drank it down. It had the desired effect on Kallie who immediately asked, "How can you drink that stuff?" Mike replied, "First of all, it has nothing to do with you, secondly, I like it and thirdly, I write with a ball point."

COURTING HUMOUR

The bride and groom decided to put *their things* together. This happened shortly after they had driven to Hartebeespoort Dam and parked under a tree. He put his hand on her thigh and started feeling it. After a while she pleaded, "...go further." So he started the car and drove to Brits. In Brits, he parked the car again. This time he kissed her and while rubbing her tummy said, "I love you."

She said, "Lower, lower."

He then lowered his voice and in a deeper voice said, "I love you, I love you."

She told this story to her bridesmaid who said, "But you hardly knew the man, weren't you afraid that he might steal your money?"
"No", said the bride, "my money was in my purse on the back seat."
Back home, he decided to propose to her but didn't know exactly how, so he turned to her and said, "Do you think that you and I could walk the road together from here on?"
She thought he meant from the car to her house and said, "Sure, I see my father is still awake, we can have coffee together."
"No! No! I meant will you marry me?"
"Oh! Is that what you meant? Of course, of course!"

TOO TENSE

Although he doesn't realise it yet, now that they're married, he not only has another mouth to feed, but another one to which he has to listen as well. He went to a psychiatrist for advice a few days ago and said, "Doctor, sometimes I feel as if I'm a Wig-Wam and sometimes I feel as if I'm a Tee-Pee, can you help me?"
"You're quite normal" said the doctor, "sometimes you're just two tents (too tense)."

A PEER IN THE POT

He was walking through the kitchen one evening and decided to take a peek into a pot on the stove. He had no sooner lifted the lid when he dropped it and stuck his fingers into his mouth. "Darling, did you burn yourself?" she asked.
"No, it just doesn't take me long to look into a pot" he said.

FRENCHMAN

A Frenchman was invited to the Silver Wedding Anniversary of a well-known couple. "I do not understand" he said, "what Silver Anniversary means."
"It means that they are celebrating 25 years of living together happily."
"Ah" said the Frenchman, smiling broadly. "Now they marry! Wonderful!"

SO EXTRAVAGANT

A Frenchman was walking past a Sandton home, when a local housewife, just getting out of her bath, decided to open the window to let in some fresh air. The window was stuck and she couldn't open it. She took a few paces back and, running forward, pushed the window so hard that it flew open. She continued straight through the window and landed head first in the refuse bin, with only her legs sticking out. At that moment the Frenchman walked passed, saw this lot and said, "Tch Tch, these South Africans are so extravagant – she is good for at least *another five years.*"

THE ROTTWEILERS

An architect had a Rottweiler and was boasting in the local pub about his dog's superior intelligence. An estate agent overheard this and claimed that his Rottweiler was even more intelligent. A civil servant sitting near-by heard their argument and soon joined in, claiming that his Rottweiler was the best.

To settle this once and for all, they decided to meet on the lawns at the Union Buildings at 10 o'clock one Sunday morning with their dogs. The architect was first, and he took a packet of biscuits from his pocket, broke them into little pieces, threw them on the lawn and said, "OK, *Sliderule*, do your stuff."

Sliderule went into action picking up all the biscuit pieces and placing them one on top of the other until he had build a perfect little model of the Union Buildings.

The estate agent was next. He also broke up a packet of biscuits, dropped the pieces onto the lawn and said to his dog, "OK, *Salescommission*, do your stuff." Well, *Salescommission* built a bridge spanning the model of the Union Buildings and then, as an encore, old *Salescommission* put up a 'For Sale' sign in front of the model.

It was now the civil servant's turn. He looked at his dog and said, "OK, *Teatime*, do your stuff." Old *Teatime* went into action immediately – he gobbled up all the biscuits, serviced the other two Rottweilers and took the afternoon off.

ARTICHOKES

Artie was the local mafia man; you could hire him to do anything. Van der Merwe phoned him up and said that he would like to get rid of his wife, Lettie, who worked at Select & Pay. They agreed that Artie would do the job for R1. The next day, Artie walked into Select & Pay, asked to see Lettie, walked up to her and choked her. As she dropped to the floor he said, "That's the end of Lettie van der Merwe." One of the other girls on the counter said, "But that's not Lettie van der Merwe! That's Lettie van der Westhuizen. Lettie van der Merwe is over there at the next counter." So Artie walked up to her and choked her as well. The next day the Pretoria News carried the headline, "Artie chokes two for R1 at Select & Pay."

TO WHOM IT MAY CONCERN

A man was advised by his doctor that he should undergo surgery for a by-pass operation. The operation was a great success, but his wife would not respond to his affections anymore. She insisted that after the major surgery that he had undergone, his heart might stop. Eventually, she agreed that if the doctor was prepared to give him a letter to the effect that sex was safe in his condition, it would be OK with her. He explained his position to his doctor and asked for a letter. The doctor said, "Certainly, what's your wife's name again?"
"Doctor, would you mind addressing the letter to, 'To whom it may concern'?"

GRANDPA

When a certain bridegroom was a little boy, he was playing on the lawn at his grandfather's home. He saw something sticking out of a hole in the lawn and tugged at it gently until eventually he pulled a long earthworm out of the ground. His grandfather looked at this lot and said to him, "If you can put that worm back into the hole, I'll give you R10". He ran into the house and came back with a can of 'Spray and Stay'. He held the worm in one hand and sprayed it thoroughly until it was stiff. He then proceeded to put it back into the hole.
While claiming his R10 from Grandpa, granddad said, "Son, I'll give you R50 if you tell me the name of that stuff."

NO CULTURE

A young man had been courting a girl for some time when she said to him, "I don't think you must come around anymore."
"Why not" he asked.

"Because my father says you have no culture."
"What!" he exclaimed, "I take you to the ballet, the opera, symphony orchestras and all that bloody rubbish and your father says I have no culture?"

BLAME THE GOVERNMENT

"Why do you want to get married?"
"So that I don't have to blame the Government for everything that goes wrong anymore."

GETTING CLEVERER AND CLEVERER

When the (bridegroom) was a little boy, he always loved to go to a rugby game with his father. One day during a big match at Loftus, the game was just getting interesting when he wanted to go to the toilet. His father told him to hold on until half-time. He managed to hold out *but only just*. Waiting in line in the Gents, men were standing about six deep. He realised that he would not make it if he waited his turn, so he simply pushed through to the front where he was able to relieve himself. He could no longer see his father and decided to just stand there and wait until his father joined him. While he waited, he did what most little boys do, he did inspection up and down the line.

Back in his seat he wanted to know from his father why some men were so well-endowed, while others seemed to have been short changed. His father said, "It's like some people are clever, son, and others are stupid." He accepted the answer unequivocally. A few days later, when his father came home from work, he told his father that he had been to the municipal swimming pool that day and that there was a beautiful girl lying on her towel wearing a bikini when a man came and lay down beside her.

He started rubbing suntan lotion on her back, and said, "Dad, I could see the man getting cleverer and cleverer!"

ORDERED RADIO BY MAIL ORDER

A rural farmer had ordered a radio by mail order. When after three months he had not yet received it, he became concerned and so decided to take a train to Cape Town, from where he had ordered it to find out what had happened to it. After waiting at a small railway siding for two days, the train arrived. He embarked and bought his ticket on board. The conductor soon realised that the farmer, who was a little backward, probably seldom went into the city. He told the farmer to look out of the window and then he would see another set of railway tracks alongside the ones that they were travelling on. "Now it is just possible" he said, "that another train travelling from Cape Town could pass us with your radio on board and you would miss it. You would then be wasting your time and money going to Cape Town."
"What on earth shall I do?" asked the farmer.
"Why don't you phone them" said the conductor.
"How do I phone them?" asked the farmer.
The conductor, realising that the farmer had probably never seen a phone before decided to have some fun.

"Come with me" he said, and took the farmer to the toilet, where he told him to sit on the floor with his legs wrapped around the toilet bowl, holding the chain in his one hand. The conductor then explained to him that he should pull the chain and then speak into the bowl. The conductor then left and went to call his colleague to come and have a look at this lot. Arriving back with his colleague, the farmer was still pulling at the chain and shouting "Hello! hello!" into the bowl. The conductor asked, "Haven't you got through yet?"
The farmer replied, "Gosh, it's raining so much in the Cape, I can't hear a word they're saying down there."

I DIDN'T KNOW YOU WERE SO RELIGIOUS

On his first date at varsity, long before he met his charming wife, the bridegroom was quite excited about his prospects with a young lady he was dating for the weekend, so he went to the local pharmacy and bought a packet of condoms. He turned back at the door and asked the pharmacist how many there were in the packet. The pharmacist said, "Three."
He said, "Then I had better take two packets."
The pharmacist said, "We do have family packs with 12 in, you know."
"OK" he said, "give me two family packs" and off he went.

Later that day, when the young lady phoned to invite him for dinner at her parents' home, he accepted. On arrival, he was seated at the dinner table and soon afterwards her father asked him to say grace. Well, he prayed until the dinner was cold and no sooner had he said amen, when he remembered an important appointment elsewhere. He apologised and asked to be excused. The young lady walked with him to his car and said, "Gosh I didn't know that you were so religious."
He said, "And I didn't know that your father was the pharmacist."

I PRAYED FOR YOU LAST NIGHT

The bridegroom was doing some missionary work for the church down at the docks when he met this young lady who was leading the sailors astray. He thought that if he could straighten her life out he would have really succeeded in doing something good. The next time down at the docks he looked her up and said, "You know, I prayed for you last night." She said, "Why didn't you phone me? My number is in the book, I would have come straight over."

INTRODUCING THE BRIDEGROOM

The bridegroom belonged to the local debating society for a while, where, he became quite a hit with his virtuosity, a talent that he will demonstrate to you when he is called upon in a few minutes time to speak to you for the first time as a married man. I am sure that he will make good use of this occasion, because now that he's married he may not get many opportunities to speak again. The debating society will always remember him for his speech on sex which he started by saying, "It gives me great pleasure."

TEACHING MY WIFE TO DRIVE

I decided that if ever my wife got a flat tyre, she should know how to change a wheel on her own. After demonstrating the whole procedure, I said to her, "OK, now let's go for a drive and put you to the test." A few miles out of town I suggested that she stop under a tree and change a wheel. She was doing very well when a car stopped alongside. The driver took one look at me sitting in the shade and shouted, "You lazy oaf! Why don't you help her?"

TARZAN

Have you ever wondered why, when Tarzan swings through the trees he shouts "Aaahwhoowhaaa!"? Well, the story goes that Jane was surrounded by lions one day and called frantically for help. Tarzan arrived in the nick of time and swinging down shouted to Jane, "Grab the rope!". With her attention focused on the lions, she grabbed the wrong rope and they continued swinging to safety with Tarzan shouting "Aaahwhooowhaaa!".

MATRIMONIAL ARGUMENT

My wife and I were having one of those matrimonial arguments the other day when I said to her, "Now let's get one thing straight between us." She replied, "That's the problem with you, all you ever think of is sex."

TALKING BALLS

I was lecturing to a class on property economics at Pretoria University, and the subject was interest rates. I had a golf ball in my pocket so I decided to use a bit of showmanship. Throwing the ball into the air and catching it, I said "What goes up must come down." One student put his hand up as if to ask a question.
I stopped, pointed at him and said, "Yes?"
He replied, "It seems *we're* talking interest rates and *you're* talking balls!"

POLITICS

Ben at one stage had political ambitions. He was driving along in his car one day when a man on a bicycle came around a corner at break-neck speed. He hit the curbstone and disappeared into a hedge in a cloud of dust. Ben stopped and went to the man's aid. "Let me help you" he said.
"No thanks, I'm all right."
"At least let me take you home, we can put your bicycle in the boot."
"Don't worry, I'll be OK."

Then Ben pulled out his trumpcard and said, "The elections are tomorrow, will you come and vote for me?"
"I fell on my *backside, not on my head*" was his reply.

TWO SEATER

I stopped in a small town in the Great Karoo to fill up and use the loo. While my car was being attended to, I walked around the back to where the loo was and found an old fashioned corrugated iron building, with its door half open. As I opened the door further to step inside, I was embarrassed to see a man already occupying the seat. "Oh, sorry" I said, and stepped back.
"Come inside" he boomed, "it's a two- seater anyway."
Sitting side by side he asked, "What are you doing in these parts?"
"I've just come to see how the land lies" I said.
"It's not the land that lies, it's those bloody estate agents" he announced.

GET THE WRONG IDEA

A wealthy Sandton housewife came home from a tea party and called Jim, the trusted housekeeper into the bedroom. Once there, she commanded, "Now Jim, take off my dress."
"Yes, ma'am."
"Now my bra and my panties, and Jim, the next time I come home and find you wearing my clothes, *you're fired*, do you understand?"

PROPERTY

Owning property these days is like having a mistress. Very desirable, very expensive to maintain and very difficult to get rid of.

REQUIRE TESTIMONIALS

The bridegroom applied for a job at Onderstepoort and they required some testimonials from his previous employer, *Glen College*, near Bloemfontein. They sent off a fax and asked whether or not they could oblige. *Glen College* replied that, "his father is the president of the local agricultural union, as was his grandfather before him. His mother is chairperson of the *Oranje Vrouevereniging*, and his uncle is the dean of the faculty for agriculture at *Bloemfontein University*. Yet another uncle is the member of parliament for the eastern Free State. The man is from a fine family."

Onderstepoort sent another fax saying, "We don't want to use him for breeding purposes, we just want to give him a job!"

RECTUM THERMOMETER

"Doctor, what are you doing with a rectum thermometer behind your ear?"
"Damn, I wonder which bum has my pencil!"

CANNOT BEAR A CHILD

If a lady cannot bear a child that does not necessarily mean that she is inconceivable or unbearable, perhaps only impregnable.

INSURANCE

"Now that you are married you will want to take out some insurance."
"Not at all, she's not the least bit dangerous."

THE PRIVATE SECTOR

The bridegroom together with other local citizens had been doing a bit of consulting work for the City Council, so the Council decided to give a party to say thanks to all the private sector people who assisted them. At the function, a large box was brought into the town hall and after the mayor's thank-you speech, the lid came off and out jumped a couple of topless waitresses. "What was it like?" I asked him.

He said, "I think it must be the first time that the City Council has ever done anything to stimulate the private sector."

THE LAW PROTECTS YOU

"Dad, why is man only allowed to have one wife?"
"Son, the law is there to protect you."

NO LAST WORDS

A family of four arrived in South Africa from England. One son settled in Cape Town and the other in Johannesburg. Five years later the parents were visiting the son in Cape Town when the father had a heart attack and died. When news got to the son in Johannesburg, he sent a telegram, "What were father's last words?"

The reply was, "Father had no last words, mother was with him to the end."

MOTHERS

I want to ask you a few questions about marriage.
"Why don't you ask my mother?"
"No, I don't want to know that much about it."

SUCH A SMALL THING

A few days ago, the bride came around to the bridegroom's home to discuss final arrangements for the wedding. The bridegroom was in the shower when she called and was unaware that she had arrived. When he had finished showering he wrapped the towel around his waist and walking through to the bedroom, his towel hooked onto a door handle. At that moment, the bride came around the corner just in time to see the towel fall to the floor, and the poor man darting in the nude to the bedroom.

The bride laughed uncontrollably for about 20 minutes. Now the bridegroom wants to know from me why she laughed so much for such a small thing.

SLOWING DOWN

Reg has slowed down a lot since I met him, I gave him a dozen oysters to eat last night – *only seven worked.*

GET THEE BEHIND ME, SATAN

My wife came home with another new dress, we hadn't paid for the last one yet. I said to her, "Couldn't you just for once have said, get thee behind me, Satan?"
"Oh darling, I did" she said, "then he whispered in my ear, 'it fits you like a dream at the back'."

TRUE LOVE

After 30 years of married life, when you wake up in the morning and your wife is in bed next to you – there are no more rosy cheeks, no more peaches and cream complexion, not quite as much sparkle in her eyes, in fact she looks more like a 'Tiger Moth' that has made a crash landing in your bed. She opens her blood-shot eyes and smiles at you and you get a warm feeling in your heart. *That is true love!*

LAWYER

Do you take this man to be your lawful wedded husband, hereinafter referred to as the defendant?

POTENTIAL MILLIONAIRE

The bridegroom is destined to become a millionaire – he can make two gallons of wine from one gallon – he simply adds water.

WHAT DO WE NEED DAD FOR?

My son asked his mother if it is true that storks bring babies.
"Yes" answered the wife.
"And is it also true that the Lord provides us with our daily bread?"
"Yes, my dear, that is also true."
"And is it true that Father Christmas brings us our presents at Christmas time?"
"Yes, son but why do you ask?"
"I was just wondering what we need Dad for."

EVOLVED FROM APES

When the bride was a little girl she went to her mother and asked, "... is it true that we evolved from apes?"
Her mother replied, "I don't know dear, I never really got to know your father's family very well."

BRIDEGROOM'S LOVE

I overheard the bridegroom say that he loves his bride so much, that if ever she wanted to leave him – he would go with her.

SWOP

"I got a dog for my wife."
"Gosh, I wish I could do a swop like that."

ANGEL

"I am married to an angel."
"How can you tell?"
"Well, she's always in the air, she has never got anything to wear and she's always *harping on something.*"

CHAINS OF WEDLOCK

The chains of wedlock are very heavy – that's why it takes two very strong people to carry them.

FINISHED

A man is incomplete until he is married and thereafter he is completely finished.

IN HEAVEN

Lovers can do no wrong because when you are in love you are in heaven – and in heaven nothing is wrong.

SUICIDE

The police could find no reason for the man's suicide – he was unmarried.

HANGING AROUND

"If I can't come and visit you anymore, then I am going to hang myself from that tree outside your home."
"No, please don't do that, you know that my father doesn't want you hanging around."

JUST MARRIED

On the first night, just before booking into the hotel the wife said, "Let's make as if we've been married for years."
"OK" said the husband, "but do you think you can carry both the suitcases?"

PAINT THE TOWN

Before marriage, every weekend you paint the town red. After marriage, you have to paint the varanda, the kitchen, the bedroom, etc.

INSIGNIFICANT DETAIL

While planning the wedding day arrangements, the bride said to her future mother-in-law, "I'm just worried that perhaps I have forgotten one small insignificant detail."
"Don't worry, my dear, I'll see to it that he gets there."

MOTHERS-IN-LAW

"I didn't mean all those nasty things I said about your family – in fact, I prefer your mother-in-law to mine."

PIGEON TURPIE

After the service, while the bridegroom was standing outside the church, some pigeons flew overhead and one dropped a turpie on his head. He turned to his bride and said, "I wonder where I can get hold of a piece of toilet paper."
She said, "Oh, don't worry, darling you will probably never find that pigeon now."

DECISIONS

When my wife and I got married, we agreed that all the small decisions would be taken by her and all the big decisions would be mine. We've been married now for 20 years and I haven't had to take a decision yet.

MARRY ME

"Will you marry me?"
"Is that all you want to say?"
"I think I have said too much already."

LAST WORD

The conversation turned to wives. Peter said, "When my wife and I have an argument, I always have the last word."
"Really?" asked an interested listener.
"Yes" came the reply, "I apologise."

IT BALANCES OUT

"I'm not at all pleased with the way your wife looks" said the doctor to the husband as he gravely emerged from the sick room.
"I'll go along with that, doc" said the husband. "She's not very good-looking, but she's a good housekeeper and she's excellent with the children, so I guess it all balances out."

A few weeks ago the bridegroom helped an elderly lady across a busy street. On the other side she thanked him and told him that she was actually a Fairy Godmother and for his kind deed he could make a wish!

He said, "I wish you would build me a highway from here to America for my exclusive use, then I could slip across in my Porsche whenever I feel like it."
The Fairy Godmother said, "I will have to take this one to my Board of Directors for approval because it exceeds my budget."

A few days later the Fairy Godmother returns and says, "My board says that it will exceed my budget for the next ten years and asked if you would kindly consider an alternative wish."

"Yes, of course" said the bridegroom, "I am getting married soon and I wish you would help me to understand the mind of a woman."
The Fairy Godmother said, "Such an unusual wish would also require the approval of my board, so I shall return in a few days' time with their answer."

A few days went by and the Fairy Godmother reappeared and asked the bridegroom, "... this highway that you want built, must it be a single or double carriageway?"

THE END